AQA Science Chemistry

New GCSE

Lawrie Ryan

Patrick Fullick

Bev Cox

John Scottow

Series Editor
Lawrie Ryan

Nelson Thornes

AQA examination questions are reproduced by permission of the Assessment and Qualifications Alliance.

Published in 2011 by:
Nelson Thornes Ltd
Delta Place
27 Bath Road
CHELTENHAM
GL53 7TH
United Kingdom

12 13 14 15 / 10 9 8 7 6 5 4

A catalogue record for this book is available from the British Library

ISBN 978 1 4085 0829 9

Cover photograph: John Feingersh/Blend Images/Corbis

Page make-up by Wearset Ltd, Boldon, Tyne and Wear

Printed in China

Photo acknowledgements

How Science Works
H1.1 Science Source/Science Photo Library; H1.2 iStockphoto; H2.1 Martyn F. Chillmaid; H3.1 James Lauritz/Digital Vision C (NT); H3.2 iStockphoto; H4.1 TEK Image/Science Photo Library; H4.2 Cordelia Molloy/Science Photo Library; H9.1 NASA; H10.1 iStockphoto; H10.SQ3 iStockphoto; H10.SQ4 Andrew Lambert Photography/Science Photo Library; H10.SQ8 Rubberball/Photolibrary.

Unit 1
C1.1.1 Charles D. Winters/Science Photo Library; C1.3.3 Martyn F. Chillmaid/Science Photo Library; C1.4.1 iStockphoto; C2.1.1 iStockphoto; C2.1.2 Last Refuge/Getty Images; C2.1.3 Alison Bowden/Fotolia; C2.2.1 Peter Arnold Images/Photolibrary; C2.2.2 iStockphoto; C2.2.3 Andrew Lambert Photography/Science Photo Library; C2.4.1 Ru Baile/Fotolia; C2.4.2 iStockphoto; C2.4.3 Cordelia Molloy/Science Photo Library; C2.5.1 Mark Thomas/Science Photo Library; C2.5.2 Digital Light Source/Photolibrary; C2.5.3a Yuri Arcurs/Fotolia; C2.5.3b Absolut/Fotolia; C2.5.3c Joetex1/Fotolia; C2.5.3d Studio Vision1/Fotolia; C2.5.3e iStockphoto; C2.5.3f iStockphoto; C2.5.3g iStockphoto; C2.5.4 iStockphoto; C2.5.5 Thomas Sztanek/Fotolia; C3.1.1 Britain on View/Photolibrary; C3.1.3 iStockphoto; C3.2.1 Luis Veiga/Getty Images; C3.2.2 Ton Kinsbergen/Science Photo Library; C3.2.3 iStockphoto; C3.2.4 iStockphoto; C3.3.1 Dmitriy Ystuyjanin/Fotolia; C3.3.2 iStockphoto; C3.3.3 Image Source/Rex Features; C3.4.1 Lee Prince/Fotolia; C3.4.3 CSIRO; C3.5.2 Jeff Greenberg/Photolibrary; C3.5.3 iStockphoto; C3.5.4 iStockphoto; C3.5.5 Michellepix/Fotolia; C3.6.2 Eco Images/Universal Images Group/Getty Images; C3.6.3 iStockphoto; C4.1.1 Tim Graham/Getty Images; C4.2.3 iStockphoto; C4.3.1 John Millar/Getty Images; C4.3.3 Copyright 2010 Photolibrary; C4.5.1 USDA; C4.5.3 Bloomberg via Getty Images; C5.1.1 Paul Rapson/Science Photo Library; C5.2.1 Cordelia Molloy/Science Photo Library; C5.2.3 Charles D. Winters/Science Photo Library; C5.3.1 Image Source/Rex Features; C5.4.1 iStockphoto; C5.4.2 Ap Photo/Josh Reynolds; C5.4.4a Pixel Shepherd/Photolibrary; C5.4.4b Northscape/Alamy; C5.5.1 Martyn F. Chillmaid/Science Photo Library; C5.5.2 Scott Sinklier/Agstockusa/Science Photo Library; C6.1.1 iStockphoto; C6.1.2 Cordelia Molloy/Science Photo Library; C6.2.1 Morphy Richards Ltd; C6.2.2 Cordelia Molloy/Science Photo Library; C6.2.4 © Rnl – Fotolia; C6.3.1 iStockphoto; C6.3.2a iStockphoto; C6.3.2b Alain Pol Ism/Science Photo Library; C6.3.3 iStockphoto; C6.4.1 Cordelia Molloy/Science Photo Library; C6.4.2 Martyn F. Chillmaid; C6.4.3 iStockphoto; C6.4.4 Garo/Phanie/Rex Features; C7.1.2 Noaa/Science Photo Library; C7.2.1 John Cancalosi/Photolibrary; C7.2.3 Canadian Press/Rex Features; C7.3.1 iStockphoto; C7.3.2 Stocktrek RF/Getty Images; C7.3.3 Georgette Douwma/Science Photo Library; C7.3.4 Penn State University/Science Photo Library; C7.4.2 Science Source/Science Photo Library; C7.4.3b. Murton/Southampton Oceanography Centre/Science Photo Library; C7.5.1 Psamtik/Fotolia; C7.5.4 H. Raguet/Eurelios/Science Photo Library; C7.6.2 Copyright 2010 Photolibrary.

Unit 2
C1.3.0 Fotolia; C1.3.1 Photolibrary; C1.4.1 Leonard Lee Rue/Science Photo Library; C1.4.6 Dirk Wiersma/Science Photo Library; C1.5.3 iStockphoto; C2.3.2 Fotolia; C2.4.1 Bloomberg/Getty Images; C2.4.3a Fotolia; C2.4.3b iStockphoto; C2.4.4 Pascal Goetgheluck/Science Photo Library; C2.5.1 Lawrence Lawry/Science Photo Library; C2.5.2 Benelux Benelux/Photolibrary; C2.5.5 Innershadows/Fotolia; C2.6.1 AFP/Getty Images; C2.6.2 Amaxim/Fotolia; C2.6.3a Pasieka/Science Photo Library; C2.6.3b Laguna Design/Science Photo Library; C3.3.1 Bloomberg/Getty Images; C3.4.1 iStockphoto; C3.6.1 Andrew Lambert Photography/Science Photo Library; C3.6.2 Sciencephotos/Alamy; C3.7.1 Martyn F. Chillmaid; C3.7.2 Charles D. Winters/Science Photo Library; C3.7.3 David Pearson/Alamy; C3.7.4a Mary Evans Picture Library; C3.7.4b Noel Hendrickson/Photolibrary; C4.1.1 Colin Marshall/FLPA; C4.2.1 Fotolia; C4.2.2 iStockphoto; C4.3.1 Age Fotostock/Photolibrary; C4.3.2 iStockphoto; C4.4.1 Cordelia Molloy/Science Photo Library; C4.5.1 Dr Keith Wheeler/Science Photo Library; C4.5.2 Sheila Terry/Science Photo Library; C4.6.1 Sabine Lubnow FLPA; C4.6.2 Copyright 2009 American Chemical Society; C4.7.1 iStockphoto; C4.7.2 iStockphoto; C4.7.3 Sian Irvine/Photolibrary; C4.8.2 Martyn F. Chillmaid/Science Photo Library; C4.8.3 Andrew Lambert Photography/Science Photo Library; C4.9.1 Martyn F. Chillmaid; C4.9.3 Fuse/Getty Images; C5.1.1a Martyn F. Chillmaid/Science Photo Library; C5.1.1b Andrew Lambert Photography/Science Photo Library; C5.3.1 Adrian Sherratt/Alamy; C5.3.2 iStockphoto; C5.4.1 iStockphoto; C5.6.1 iStockphoto; C5.7.2 iStockphoto; C5.8.1 iStockphoto, C5.8.2 Aberenyi/Fotolia.

Unit 3
C1.1.2 Sheila Terry/Science Photo Library; C1.1.3 Science Photo Library; C1.1.4 CCI Archives/Science Photo Library; C1.3.2 Martyn F. Chillmaid/Science Photo Library; C1.3.3 Martyn F. Chillmaid; C1.4.3 Dirk Wiersma/Science Photo Library; C2.1.1 iStockphoto; C2.1.2 Rebvt/Fotolia; C2.1.3 iStockphoto; C2.2.1 Pink Sun Media/Alamy; C2.3.1 iStockphoto; C2.3.2 iStockphoto; C2.3.3 Cardoso Cardoso/Bsip Medical/Photolibrary; C2.4.2 Martyn F. Chillmaid/Science Photo Library; C2.5.2 DenGuy/IstockPhoto; C2.5.3 Trevor Clifford Photography/Science Photo Library; C2.5.4 Martyn F. Chillmaid/Science Photo Library C3.1.1 Fotolia; C3.1.2 iStockphoto; C3.5.1 Paul Buck/EPA/Corbis; C3.5.2 Dane Andrew/CorbisNews; C3.5.3 Toby Melville/Reuters/Corbis; C3.6.2 Bettman/Corbis; C4.1.1 David Taylor/Science Photo Library; C4.1.2 Andrew Lambert Photography/Science Photo Library; C4.2.2 Science Photo Library; C4.2.3 Charles D. Winters/Science Photo Library; C4.3.3 Andrew Lambert Photography/Science Photo Library; C4.5.1 Maximilian Stock Ltd/Science Photo Library; C4.5.5 Terra/Corbis; C4.8.1 ICI; C4.9.1 Maximilian Stock Ltd/Science Photo Library; C5.1.4 Martyn F. Chillmaid/Science Photo Library; C5.2.1 iStockphoto; C5.2.2 Andrew Lambert Photography/Science Photo Library; C5.3.2 Craig Lovell/Agstockusa/Science Photo Library; C5.4.1 Michael Hilgert/AgeFotoStock/Photolibrary; C5.4.2 PAPhotos; C5.4.3 Bionafta.

Chemistry Contents

Welcome to AQA GCSE Chemistry!

This book has been written for you by the people who will be marking your exams, very experienced teachers and subject experts. It covers everything you need to know for your exams and is packed full of features to help you achieve the very best that you can.

Questions in yellow boxes check that you understand what you are learning as you go along. The answers are all within the text so if you don't know the answer, you can go back and reread the relevant section.

Figure 1 Many diagrams are as important for you to learn as the text, so make sure you revise them carefully.

Key words are highlighted in the text. You can look them up in the glossary at the back of the book if you are not sure what they mean.

Where you see this icon, you will know that this part of the topic involves How Science Works – a really important part of your GCSE and an interesting way to understand 'how science works' in real life.

Where you see this icon, there are supporting electronic resources in our Kerboodle online service.

Learning objectives

Each topic begins with key questions that you should be able to answer by the end of the lesson.

AQA Examiner's tip

Hints from the examiners who will mark your exams, giving you important advice on things to remember and what to watch out for.

??? Did you know ...?

There are lots of interesting, and often strange, facts about science. This feature tells you about many of them.

∞ links

Links will tell you where you can find more information about what you are learning.

Practical

This feature helps you become familiar with key practicals. It may be a simple introduction, a reminder or the basis for a practical in the classroom.

Activity

An activity is linked to a main lesson and could be a discussion or task in pairs, groups or by yourself.

Anything in the Higher Tier boxes must be learned by those sitting the Higher Tier exam. If you'll be sitting the Foundation Tier, these boxes can be missed out.

The same is true for any other places which are marked Higher or [H].

Maths skills

This feature highlights the maths skills that you will need for your GCSE Chemistry exams with short, visual explanations.

Summary questions

These questions give you the chance to test whether you have learned and understood everything in the topic. If you get any wrong, go back and have another look.

And at the end of each chapter you will find …

Summary questions

These will test you on what you have learned throughout the whole chapter, helping you to work out what you have understood and where you need to go back and revise.

AQA Examination-style questions

These questions are examples of the types of questions you will answer in your actual GCSE exam, so you can get lots of practice during your course.

Key points

At the end of the topic are the important points that you must remember. They can be used to help with revision and summarising your knowledge.

How does science work? ⓚ

Learning objectives

- What is meant by 'How Science Works'?
- What is a prediction and why should you make one?
- What is a hypothesis?
- How can you investigate a problem scientifically?

∞ **links**
You can find out more about your ISA by looking at H10 The ISA at the end of this chapter.

This first chapter looks at 'How Science Works'. It is an important part of your GCSE because the ideas introduced here will crop up throughout your course. You will be expected to collect scientific **evidence** and to understand how we use evidence. These concepts will be assessed as the major part of your internal school assessment.

You will take one or more 45-minute tests. These tests are based on **data** you have collected previously plus data supplied for you in the test. They are called **Investigative Skills Assignments (ISA)**. The ideas in 'How Science Works' will also be assessed in your examinations.

How science works for us

Science works for us all day, every day. You do not need to know how a mobile phone works to enjoy sending text messages. But, think about how you started to use your mobile phone or your television remote control. Did you work through pages of instructions? Probably not!

You knew that pressing the buttons would change something on the screen (**knowledge**). You played around with the buttons, to see what would happen (**observation**). You had a guess based on your knowledge and observations at what you thought might be happening (**prediction**) and then tested your idea (**experiment**).

Perhaps 'How Science Works' should really be called 'How Scientists Work'.

Science moves forward by slow, steady steps. When a genius such as Einstein comes along, it takes a giant leap. Those small steps build on knowledge and experience that we already have.

The steps don't always lead in a straight line, starting with an observation and ending with a conclusion. More often than not you find yourself going round in circles, but each time you go around the loop you gain more knowledge and so can make better predictions.

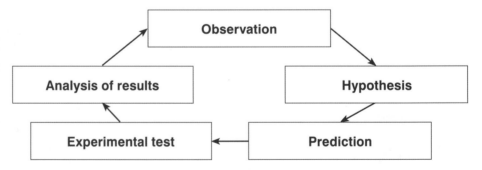

Each small step is important in its own way. It builds on the body of knowledge that we have. In 1675 a German chemist tried to extract gold from urine. He must have thought that there was a connection between the two colours. He was wrong. But after a while, with a terrible stench coming from his laboratory, the urine began to glow.

He had discovered phosphorus. Phosphorus catches fire easily. A Swedish scientist worked out how to manufacture phosphorus without the smell of urine. That is why most matches these days are manufactured in Sweden.

Figure 1 Albert Einstein was a genius, but he worked through scientific problems in the same way as you will in your GCSE

Activity

Investigating fireworks

Fireworks must be safe to light. Therefore you need a fuse that will last long enough to give you time to get well out of the way.

- Fuses can be made by dipping a special type of cotton into a mixture of two chemicals. One chemical (A) reacts by burning; the other (B) doesn't.
- The chemicals stick to the cotton. Once it is lit, the cotton will continue to burn, setting the firework off. The concentrations of the two chemicals will affect how quickly the fuse burns.
- In groups, discuss how you could work out the correct concentrations of the chemicals to use. You want the fuse to last long enough for you to get out of the way. However, you don't want it to burn so long that we all get bored waiting for the firework to go off!

You can use the following headings to discuss your investigation. One person should be writing your ideas down, so that you can discuss them with the rest of the class.

- What prediction can you make about the concentration of the two chemicals (A and B) and the fuse?
- What would you vary in each test? This is called the independent variable.
- What would you measure to judge the effect of varying the independent variable? This is called the dependent variable.
- What would you need to keep unchanged to make this a fair test? These are called control variables.
- Write a plan for your investigation.

Figure 2 Fireworks

Key points

- **Observations** are often the starting point for an investigation.
- A **hypothesis** is a proposal intended to explain certain facts or observations.
- A **prediction** is an intelligent guess, based on some **knowledge**.
- An **experiment** is a way of testing your prediction.

Summary questions

1 Copy and complete this paragraph using the following words:

experiment knowledge conclusion prediction observation

You have learned before that a cup of tea loses heat if it is left standing. This is a piece of _____ . You make an _____ that dark-coloured cups will cool faster. So you make a _____ that if you have a black cup, this will cool fastest of all. You carry out an _____ to get some results, and from these you make a _____ .

Fundamental ideas about how science works

Learning objectives

- How do you spot when an opinion is not based on good science?

- What is the importance of continuous and categoric variables?

- What does it mean to say that evidence is valid?

- What is the difference between a result being repeatable and a result being reproducible?

- How can two sets of data be linked?

Science is too important for us to get it wrong

Sometimes it is easy to spot when people try to use science poorly. Sometimes it can be funny. You might have seen adverts claiming to give your hair 'body' or sprays that give your feet 'lift'!

On the other hand, poor scientific practice can cost lives.

Some years ago a company sold the drug thalidomide to people as a sleeping pill. Research was carried out on animals to see if it was safe. The research did not include work on pregnant animals. The **opinion** of the people in charge was that the animal research showed the drug could be used safely with humans.

Then the drug was also found to help ease morning sickness in pregnant women. Unfortunately, doctors prescribed it to many women, resulting in thousands of babies being born with deformed limbs. It was far from safe.

These are very difficult decisions to make. You need to be absolutely certain of what the science is telling you.

> **a** Why was the opinion of the people in charge of developing thalidomide based on poor science?

AQA Examiner's tip

Read a newspaper article or watch the news on TV. Ask yourself whether any research presented is valid. Ask yourself whether you can trust that person's opinion and why.

Deciding on what to measure: variables

Variables are physical, chemical or biological quantities or characteristics.

In an investigation, you normally choose one thing to change or vary. This is called the **independent variable**.

When you change the independent variable, it may cause something else to change. This is called the **dependent variable**.

A **control variable** is one that is kept the same and is not changed during the investigation.

You need to know about two different types of these variables:

- A **categoric variable** is one that is best described by a label (usually a word). The 'colour of eyes' is a categoric variable, e.g. blue or brown eyes.

- A **continuous variable** is one that we measure, so its value could be any number. Temperature (as measured by a thermometer or temperature sensor) is a continuous variable, e.g. 37.6 °C, 45.2 °C. Continuous variables can have values (called quantities) that can be found by making measurements (e.g. light intensity, flow rate, etc.).

> **b** Imagine you were testing the energy given out in three different reactions (A, B and C). Would it be best to say **i** reactions A and B felt warm, but C felt hot, or **ii** reaction C got hottest, followed by A and finally B, or **iii** the rise in temperature in reaction C was 31 °C, in A it was 16 °C and in B it was 14 °C?

Figure 1 Student recording a range of temperatures – an example of a continuous variable

Making your evidence repeatable, reproducible and valid

When you are designing an investigation you must make sure that other people can get the same results as you. This makes the evidence you collect **reproducible**. This is more likely to happen if you repeat measurements and get consistent results.

A measurement is repeatable if the original experimenter repeats the investigation using the same method and equipment and obtains the same results.

A measurement is reproducible if the investigation is repeated by another person, or by using different equipment or techniques, and the same results are obtained.

You must also make sure you are measuring the actual thing you want to measure. If you don't, your data can't be used to answer your original question. This seems very obvious but it is not always quite so easy. You need to make sure that you have controlled as many other variables as you can, so that no one can say that your investigation is not **valid**. A measurement is valid if it measures what it is supposed to be measuring, with an appropriate level of performance.

> **c** State one way in which you can show that your results are valid.

How might an independent variable be linked to a dependent variable?

Looking for a link between your independent and dependent variables is very important. The pattern of your graph or bar chart can often help you to see whether there is a link.

But beware! There may not be a link! If your results seem to show that there is no link, don't be afraid to say so. Look at Figure 2.

The points on the top graph show a clear pattern, but the bottom graph shows random scatter.

AQA *Examiner's tip*

When designing your investigation you should always try to measure continuous data whenever you can. This is not always possible, so then you have to use a label (categoric variable). You might still be able to put the variables in an order so that you can spot a pattern. For example, you could describe flow rate as 'fast flowing', 'steady flow' or 'slow flowing'.

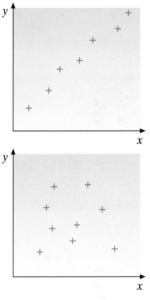

Figure 2 Which graph shows that there might be a link between x and y?

?₂? *Did you know ...?*

At any time there are only about 20 atoms of francium in the entire planet. How do we know that this data is valid?

Summary questions

1 Students were asked to find the solubility of three different solids – D, E and F. Name each of the following types of dependent variable described by the students:

  a D and E were 'soluble', whereas F was 'insoluble'.

  b 0 g of F dissolved in 100 cm³ of water, 30.2 g of D dissolved in 100 cm³ of water, 25.9 g of F dissolved in 100 cm³ of water.

2 Some people believe that the artificial sweetener aspartame causes headaches and dizziness. Do you trust these opinions? What would convince you not to use aspartame?

Key points

- Be on the lookout for non-scientific opinions.

- Continuous data give more information than other types of data.

- Check that evidence is repeatable, reproducible and valid.

Starting an investigation

Learning objectives

- How can you use your scientific knowledge to observe the world around you?

- How can you use your observations to make a hypothesis?

- How can you make predictions and start to design an investigation?

Figure 1 A rusting lock

Observation

As humans we are sensitive to the world around us. We can use our senses to detect what is happening. As scientists we use observations to ask questions. We can only ask useful questions if we know something about the observed event. We will not have all of the answers, but we know enough to start asking relevant questions.

If we observe that the weather has been hot today, we would not ask if it was due to global warming. If the weather was hotter than normal for several years, we could ask that question. We know that global warming takes many years to show its effect.

When you are designing an investigation you have to observe carefully which variables are likely to have an effect.

> **a** Would it be reasonable to ask whether the iron in Figure 1 is rusting because of acid rain? Discuss your answer.

An owner of a house noticed that the driveway up to the house had cracks in the concrete on the left side of the driveway (observation). He was concerned because the driveway had only been laid for ten weeks. The work had been done in December. Before the builder came to look at it, the owner thought of a few questions to ask the builder:

- Did the builder have the correct amount of water in the concrete?
- Did the builder use the correct amount of cement?
- Could it be the car that was causing the damage?
- Did the builder dig the foundations deep enough?
- Did the builder put the same depth of foundations on both sides?
- Could the frost have caused the damage?
- Could the bushes growing next to the drive have caused the problem?

> **b** Discuss all of these good ideas and choose three that are the most likely.

Observations, backed up by really creative thinking and good scientific knowledge, can lead to a **hypothesis**.

Testing scientific ideas

Scientists always try to think of ways to explain how things work or why they behave in the way that they do.

After their observations, they use their understanding of science to come up with an idea that could explain what is going on. This idea is sometimes called a hypothesis. They use this idea to make a prediction. A prediction is like a guess, but it is not just a wild guess – it is based on previous understanding.

A scientist will say, 'If it works the way I think it does, I should be able to change **this** (the independent variable) and **that** will happen (the dependent variable).'

Predictions are what make science so powerful. They mean that we can work out rules that tell us what will happen in the future. For example, a weather forecaster can use knowledge and understanding to predict **wind** speeds. Knowing this, sailors and windsurfers can decide whether it would be a good day to enjoy their sport.

Knowledge of energy transfer could lead to an idea that the insides of chips cook by energy being conducted from the outside. You might predict that small, thinly sliced chips will cook faster than large, fat chips.

Figure 2 Which cook faster? Small, thinly sliced chips or larger, fat chips?

> **c** Look at the photograph in Figure 2. How could you test your prediction about how fast chips cook?

Not all predictions are correct. If scientists find that the prediction doesn't work, it's back to the drawing board! They either amend their original idea or think of a completely new one.

Starting to design a valid investigation

observation ✛ **knowledge** ⟹ **hypothesis** ⟹ **prediction** ⟹ **investigation**

We can test a prediction by carrying out an **investigation**. You, as the scientist, predict that there is a relationship between two variables.

The independent variable is one that is selected and changed by you, the investigator. The dependent variable is measured for each change in your independent variable. Then all other variables become control variables, kept constant so that your investigation is a fair test.

If your measurements are going to be accepted by other people, they must be valid. Part of this is making sure that you are really measuring the effect of changing your chosen variable. For example, if other variables aren't controlled properly, they might be affecting the data collected.

Figure 3 Darren investigating the temperature change

> **d** Look at Figure 3. Darren was investigating the temperature change when adding anhydrous copper sulfate to water. He used a test tube for the reaction. What is wrong here?

Summary questions

1 Copy and complete this paragraph using the following words:

controlled   dependent   independent   knowledge
prediction   hypothesis

An observation linked with scientific .... can be used to make a .... A .... links an .... variable to a .... variable. All other variables need to be ....

2 What is the difference between a prediction and a guess?

3 Imagine you were testing whether the concentration of the reactants affects the rate of reaction. The reaction might cause the solution to get hot.
   a How could you monitor the temperature?
   b What other control variables can you think of that might affect the results?

Key points

- Observation is often the starting point for an investigation.

- Testing predictions can lead to new scientific understanding.

- You must design investigations that produce valid results if you are to be believed.

H6

Making measurements

Learning objectives

- Why do results always vary?

- How do you choose instruments that will give you accurate results?

- What do we mean by the 'resolution' of an instrument?

- What is the difference between a systematic error and a random error?

- How does human error affect results and what do you do with anomalies?

Using instruments

Try measuring the temperature of a beaker of water using a digital thermometer. Do you always get the same result? Probably not! So can we say that any measurement is absolutely correct?

In any experiment there will be doubts about actual measurements.

When you choose an instrument you need to know that it will give you the accuracy that you want. You need to be confident that it is giving a true reading.

If you have used an electric water bath, would you trust the temperature on the dial? How do you know it is the true temperature? You could use a very expensive thermometer to calibrate your water bath. The expensive thermometer is more likely to show the true temperature. But can you really be sure it is accurate?

Instruments that measure the same thing can have different sensitivities. The **resolution** of an instrument refers to the smallest change in a value that can be detected. This is one factor that determines the precision of your measurements.

Choosing the wrong scale can cause you to miss important data or make silly conclusions. We would not measure the length of a chemical bond in metres, we would use nanometres.

a Match the following weighing machines to their best use:

Used to measure	Resolution of weighing machine
Sodium chloride in a packet of cornflakes	micrograms
Cornflakes delivered to a supermarket	milligrams
Vitamin D in a packet of cornflakes	grams
Sugar added to a bowl of cornflakes	kilograms

Errors

Even when an instrument is used correctly, the results can still show differences.

Results may differ because of **random error**. This is most likely to be due to a poor measurement being made. It could be due to not carrying out the method consistently.

If you repeat your measurements several times and then calculate a mean, you will reduce the effect of random errors.

The **error** might be a **systematic error**. This means that the method was carried out consistently but an error was being repeated. A systematic error will make your readings be spread about some value other than the true value. This is because your results will differ from the true value by a consistent amount each time a measurement is made.

AQA Examiner's tip

If you are asked what may have caused an error, never answer simply '**human error**' – you won't get any marks for this. You need to say what the experimenter may have done to cause the error, or give more detail, e.g. 'Human reaction time might have caused an error in the timing when using a stopwatch.'

No number of repeats can do anything about systematic errors. If you think that you have a systematic error, you need to repeat using a different set of equipment or a different technique. Then compare your results and spot the difference!

A **zero error** is one kind of systematic error. Suppose that you were trying to measure the length of your desk with a metre rule, but you hadn't noticed that someone had sawn off half a centimetre from the end of the ruler. It wouldn't matter how many times you repeated the measurement, you would never get any nearer to the true value.

Check out these two sets of data that were taken from the investigation that Matt did. He tested five different oils. The bottom row is the time calculated from knowing the viscosity of the different oils:

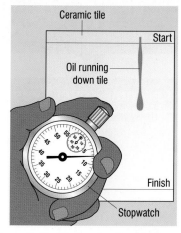

Figure 1 Matt timing the flow of oil

Type of oil used	A	B	C	D	E
Time taken to flow down tile (seconds)	23.2	45.9	49.5	62.7	75.9
	24.1	36.4	48.7	61.5	76.1
Calculated time (seconds)	18.2	30.4	42.5	55.6	70.7

b Discuss whether there is any evidence of random error in these results.

c Discuss whether there is any evidence of systematic error in these results.

Anomalies

Anomalous results are clearly out of line. They are not those that are due to the natural variation you get from any measurement. These should be looked at carefully. There might be a very interesting reason why they are so different. You should always look for anomalous results and discard them before you calculate a mean, if necessary.

- If anomalies can be identified while you are doing an investigation, it is best to repeat that part of the investigation.
- If you find anomalies after you have finished collecting data for an investigation, they must be discarded.

Summary questions

1 Copy and complete this paragraph using the following words:

accurate discarded random resolution systematic use variation

There will always be some .... in results. You should always choose the best instruments that you can in order to get the most .... results. You must know how to .... the instrument properly. The .... of an instrument refers to the smallest change that can be detected. There are two types of error – .... and .... Anomalies due to random error should be ....

2 What kind of error will most likely occur in the following situations?
  a Asking everyone in the class to measure the length of the bench.
  b Using a ruler that has a piece missing from the zero end.

H7

Presenting data

Learning objectives

- How do we calculate the mean from a set of data?
- How do you use tables of results?
- What is the range of the data?
- How do you display your data?

Figure 1 Student using an oxygen meter

For this section you will be working with data from this investigation:

Mel took a litre (1 dm³) of tap water. She shook it vigorously for exactly 2 minutes. She tried to get as much oxygen to dissolve in it as possible.

Then she took the temperature of the water. She immediately tested the oxygen concentration, using an oxygen meter.

Tables

Tables are really good for getting your results down quickly and clearly. You should design your table **before** you start your investigation.

Your table should be constructed to fit in all the data to be collected. It should be fully labelled, including units.

You may want to have extra columns for repeats, calculations of means or calculated values.

Checking for anomalies

While filling in your table of results you should be constantly looking for anomalies.

- Check to see whether any reading in a set of repeat readings is significantly different from the others.
- Check to see whether the pattern you are getting as you change the independent variable is what you expected.

Remember, a result that looks anomalous should be checked out to see whether it really is a poor reading.

Planning your table

Mel had decided on the values for her independent variable. We always put these in the first column of a table. The dependent variable goes in the second column. Mel will find its values as she carries out the investigation.

So she could plan a table like this:

Temperature of water (°C)	Concentration of oxygen (mg/dm³)
5	
10	
16	
20	
28	

Or like this:

Temperature of water (°C)	5	10	16	20	28
Concentration of oxygen (mg/dm³)					

All she had to do in the investigation was to write the correct numbers in the second column to complete the top table.

Mel's results are shown in the alternative format in the table below:

Temperature of water (°C)	5	10	16	20	28
Concentration of oxygen (mg/dm³)	12.8	11.3	9.9	9.1	7.3

The range of the data

Pick out the maximum and the minimum values and you have the range of a variable. You should always quote these two numbers when asked for a range. For example, the range of the dependent variable is between 7.3 mg/dm^3 (the lowest value) and 12.8 mg/dm^3 (the highest value) – and don't forget to include the units!

a What is the range for the independent variable and for the dependent variable in Mel's set of data?

Maths skills

The mean of the data

Often you have to find the **mean** of each repeated set of measurements. The first thing you should do is to look for any anomalous results. If you find any, miss these out of the calculation. Then add together the remaining measurements and divide by how many there are.

For example:

● Mel takes four readings, 15 mg/dm^3, 12 mg/dm^3, 29 mg/dm^3, 15 mg/dm^3

● 29 mg/dm^3 is an anomalous result and so is missed out. So 15 + 12 + 15 = 42

● 42 divided by three (the number of valid results) = **14 mg/dm^3**

The repeat values and mean can be recorded as shown below:

Temperature of water (°C)	Concentration of oxygen (mg/dm³)			
	1st test	2nd test	3rd test	Mean
0	15	12	15	14

Displaying your results

Bar charts

If one of your variables is categoric, you should use a **bar chart**.

Line graphs

If you have a continuous independent and a continuous dependent variable, a **line graph** should be used. Plot the points as small 'plus' signs (+).

Summary questions

1 Copy and complete this paragraph using the following words:

categoric continuous mean range

The maximum and minimum values show the .... of the data. The sum of all the values in a set of repeat readings divided by the total number of these repeat values gives the .... Bar charts are used when you have a .... independent variable and a continuous dependent variable. Line graphs are used when you have .... independent and dependent variables.

2 Draw a graph of Mel's results from the bottom of the previous page.

H8   Using data to draw conclusions

Learning objectives

- How do we best use charts and graphs to identify patterns?

- What are the possible relationships we can identify from charts and graphs?

- How do we draw conclusions from relationships?

- How can we decide if our results are good and our conclusions are valid?

Identifying patterns and relationships

Now that you have a bar chart or a line graph of your results you can begin to look for patterns. You must have an open mind at this point.

First, there could still be some anomalous results. You might not have picked these out earlier. How do you spot an anomaly? It must be a significant distance away from the pattern, not just within normal variation. If you do have any anomalous results plotted on your graph, circle these and ignore them when drawing the **line of best fit**.

Now look at your graph. Is there a pattern that you can see? When you have decided, draw a line of best fit that shows this pattern.

A line of best fit is a kind of visual averaging process. You should draw the line so that it leaves as many points slightly above the line as there are points below. In other words it is a line that steers a middle course through the field of points.

The vast majority of results that you get from continuous data require a line of best fit.

Remember, a line of best fit can be a straight line or it can be a curve – you have to decide from your results.

You need to consider whether your graph shows a linear **relationship**. This simply means, can you be confident about drawing a straight line of best fit on your graph? If the answer is yes – is this line positive or negative?

> **a** Say whether graphs **i** and **ii** in Figure 1 show a positive or a negative linear relationship.

Look at the graph in Figure 2. It shows a positive linear relationship. It also goes through the origin (0,0). We call this a **directly proportional** relationship.

Your results might also show a curved line of best fit. These can be predictable, complex or very complex! Look at Figure 3 below.

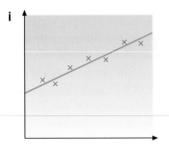

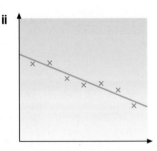

Figure 1 Graphs showing linear relationships

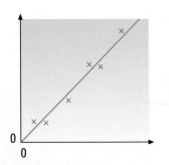

Figure 2 Graph showing a directly proportional relationship

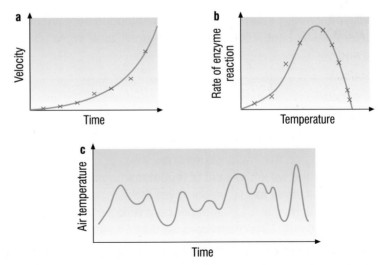

Figure 3 a Graph showing predictable results **b** Graph showing complex results **c** Graph showing very complex results

Drawing conclusions

If there is a pattern to be seen (for example as one variable gets bigger the other also gets bigger), it may be that:

- changing one has caused the other to change
- the two are related, but one is not necessarily the cause of the other.

Your conclusion must go no further than the evidence that you have.

Activity

Looking at relationships

Some people think that watching too much television can cause an increase in violence.

The table shows the number of television sets in the UK for four different years, and the number of murders committed in those years.

Year	Number of televisions (millions)	Number of murders
1970	15	310
1980	25	500
1990	42	550
2000	60	750

Plot a graph to show the relationship.

- Do you think this proves that watching television causes violence? Explain your answer.

Poor science can often happen if a wrong decision is made here. Newspapers have said that living near electricity substations can cause cancer. All that scientists would say is that there is possibly an association.

Evaluation

You will often be asked to evaluate either the method of the investigation or the conclusion that has been reached. Ask yourself: Could the method have been improved? Is the conclusion that has been made a valid one?

Summary questions

1 Copy and complete this paragraph using the following words:

anomalous   complex   directly   negative   positive

Lines of best fit can be used to identify .... results. Linear relationships can be .... or .... If a straight line goes through the origin of a graph, the relationship is .... proportional. Often a line of best fit is a curve which can be predictable or ....

2 Nasma found a newspaper article about nanoscience. Nanoparticles are used for many things, including perfumes.

There was increasing evidence that inhaled nanoparticles could cause lung inflammation. [quote from Professor Ken Donaldson]

Discuss the type of experiment and the data you would expect to see to support this conclusion.

AQA *Examiner's tip*

When you read scientific claims, think carefully about the evidence that should be there to back up the claim.

Key points

- Drawing lines of best fit helps us to study the relationship between variables.
- The possible relationships are linear, positive and negative, directly proportional, predictable and complex curves.
- Conclusions must go no further than the data available.
- The reproducibility of data can be checked by looking at other similar work done by others, perhaps on the internet. It can also be checked by using a different method or by others checking your method.

<table>
<tr><td>

H9

</td><td>

Scientific evidence and society

</td></tr>
</table>

Learning objectives

- How can science encourage people to trust its research?
- How might bias affect people's judgement of science?
- Can politics influence judgements about science?
- Do you have to be a professor to be believed?

Now you have reached a conclusion about a piece of scientific research. So what is next? If it is pure research, your fellow scientists will want to look at it very carefully. If it affects the lives of ordinary people, society will also want to examine it closely.

You can help your cause by giving a balanced account of what you have found out. It is much the same as any argument you might have. If you make ridiculous claims, nobody will believe anything you have to say.

Be open and honest. If you only tell part of the story, someone will want to know why! Equally, if somebody is only telling you part of the truth, you cannot be confident about anything they say.

a An advert for a breakfast cereal claims that it has 'extra folic acid'. What information is missing? Is it important?

You must be on the lookout for people who might be biased when presenting scientific evidence. Some scientists are paid by companies to do research. When you are told that a certain product is harmless, just check out who is telling you.

b Bottles of perfume spray contain this advice: 'This finished product has not been tested on animals.' Why might you mistrust this statement?

STAR IN SCANDAL SHOCK

We Find Out What They Don't Want You To Know... And WE TELL YOU!

MOBILE PHONE TUMOUR RISK?

Swedish researchers found that the risk of developing an ear tumour increased if you used a mobile phone. The study was of 750 people. This type of tumour affects one in 100 000 people and the risk increased four times if you used the phone for more than 10 years.

A spoke...
that

??? Did you know ... ?

A scientist who rejected the idea of a causal link between smoking and lung cancer was later found to be being paid by a tobacco company.

Suppose you wanted to know about the pollution effects of burning waste in a local incinerator. Would you ask the scientist working for the incinerator company or one working in the local university?

We also have to be very careful in reaching judgements according to who is presenting scientific evidence to us. For example, if the evidence might provoke public or political problems, it might be played down.

Equally, others might want to exaggerate the findings. They might make more of the results than the evidence suggests. Take as an example the data available on animal research. Animal liberation followers may well present the *same* evidence completely differently to pharmaceutical companies wishing to develop new drugs.

AQA Examiner's tip

If you are asked about bias in scientific evidence, there are two types:

- the measuring instruments may have introduced a bias because they were not calibrated correctly
- the scientists themselves may have a biased opinion (e.g. if they are paid by a company to promote their product).

c Check out some websites on limestone quarrying in the National Parks. Get the opinions of the environmentalists and those of the quarrying companies. Try to identify any political bias there might be in their opinions.

The status of the experimenter may place more weight on evidence. Suppose a quarrying company wants to convince an enquiry that it is perfectly reasonable to site a quarry in remote moorland in the UK. The company will choose the most eminent scientist in that field who is likely to support them. The small local community might not be able to afford an eminent scientist. The enquiry needs to be very careful to make a balanced judgement.

Science can often lead to the development of new materials or techniques. Sometimes these cause a problem for society where hard choices have to be made.

Scientists can give us the answers to many questions, but not to every question. Scientists have a contribution to make to a debate, but so do others such as environmentalists, economists and politicians.

The limitations of science

Science can help us in many ways but it cannot supply all the answers. We are still finding out about things and developing our scientific knowledge. For example, the Hubble telescope has helped us to revise our ideas about the beginnings of the universe.

There are some questions that we cannot answer, maybe because we do not have enough reproducible, repeatable and valid evidence. For example, research into the causes of cancer still needs much work to be done to provide data.

There are some questions that science cannot answer at all. These tend to be questions where beliefs, opinions and ethics are important. For example, science can suggest what the universe was like when it was first formed, but cannot answer the question of why it was formed.

BIODIESEL

The Fuel of the Future?

The demand for palm oil has grown tremendously in the last few years. It is used in many food products like margarine and chocolate, in cosmetics, and increasingly for making biodiesel.

Some scientists say that it is the answer to the dwindling supplies of crude oil because palm oil is a renewable resource.

Other people say that planting millions of acres of palm trees is destroying natural habitats such as rainforests and peat bogs.

Figure 1 The Hubble space telescope can look deep into space and tell us things about the universe's beginning from the formations of early galaxies

Summary questions

1 Copy and complete this paragraph using the following words:

status   balanced   bias   political

Evidence from scientific investigations should be given in a .... way. It must be checked for any .... from the experimenter. Evidence can be given too little or too much weight if it is of .... significance. The .... of the experimenter is likely to influence people in their judgement of the evidence.

2 Collect some newspaper articles to show how scientific evidence is used. Discuss in groups whether these articles are honest and fair representations of the science. Consider whether they carry any bias.

3 Petcoke is a high carbon product from refined oil. It can be used in power stations and cement works. Owners of the Drax power station, which is running a trial use of the fuel, claim that it is cheaper than coal and can be used without harmful effects. Other groups claim that it is 'dirty fuel' and will cause environmental and health problems. Suppose you were living near Drax power station. Who would you trust to tell you whether petcoke was a safe fuel? Explain your answer.

Key points

- Scientific evidence must be presented in a balanced way that points out clearly how valid the evidence is.

- The evidence must not contain any bias from the experimenter.

- The evidence must be checked to appreciate whether there has been any political influence.

- The status of the experimenter can influence the weight placed on the evidence.

H10

The ISA

Learning objectives

- How do you write a plan?
- How do you make a risk assessment?
- What is a hypothesis?
- How do you make a conclusion?

There are several different stages to the ISA.

Stage 1

Your teacher will tell you the problem that you are going to investigate, and you will have to develop your own hypothesis. They will also set the problem in a context – in other words, where in real life your investigation could be useful. You should have a discussion about it, and talk about different ways in which you might solve the problem. Your teacher should show you the equipment that you can use, and you should research one or two possible methods for carrying out an experiment to test the hypothesis. You should also research the context and do a risk assessment for your practical work. You will be allowed to make one side of notes on this research, which you can take into the written part of the ISA.

Figure 1 Doing practical work allows you to develop the skills needed to do well in the ISA

You should be allowed to handle the equipment and you may be allowed to carry out a preliminary experiment.

Make sure that you understand what you have to do – now is the time to ask questions if you are not sure.

AQA Examiner's tip

When you are making a blank table or drawing a graph or bar chart, make sure that you use full headings, e.g.

- 'the length of the leaf', **not** just 'length'
- 'the time taken for the reaction', **not** just 'time'
- 'the height from which the ball was dropped', **not** just 'height'

and don't forget to include any units.

⚙ How Science Works

Section 1 of the ISA

At the end of this stage, you will answer Section 1 of the ISA. You will need to:

- develop a hypothesis
- identify one or more variables that you need to control
- describe how you would carry out the main experiment
- identify possible hazards and say what you would do to reduce any risk
- make a blank table ready for your results.

a What features should you include in your written plan?
b What should you include in your blank table?

Stage 2

This is where you carry out the experiment and get some results. Don't worry too much about spending a long time getting fantastically accurate results – it is more important to get some results that you can analyse.

After you have got results, you will have to compare your results with those of others. You will also have to draw a graph or a bar chart.

c How do you decide whether you should draw a bar chart or a line graph?

Stage 3

This is where you answer Section 2 of the ISA. Section 2 of the ISA is all about your own results, so make sure that you look at your table and graph when you are answering this section. To get the best marks you will need to quote some data from your results.

How Science Works

Section 2 of the ISA

In this section you will need to:

- say what you were trying to find out
- compare your results with those of others, saying whether you think they are similar or different
- analyse data that is given in the paper. This data will be in the same topic area as your investigation
- use ideas from your own investigation to answer questions about this data
- write a conclusion
- compare your conclusion with the hypothesis you have tested.

You may need to change or even reject your hypothesis in response to your findings.

Key points

- When you are writing the plan make sure that you include details about:
  – the range and interval of the independent variable
  – the control variables
  – the number of repeats.

- Try to put down at least two possible hazards, and say how you are going to minimise the risk from them.

- Look carefully at the hypothesis that you are given – this should give you a good clue about how to do the experiment.

- Always refer back to the hypothesis when you are writing your conclusion.

Summary questions

1 Copy and complete the paragraph using the words below:

control   independent   dependent

When writing a plan, you need to state the variable that you are deliberately going to change, called the .... variable. You also need to say what you expect will change because of this; this is called the .... variable. You must also say what .... variables you will keep constant in order to make it a fair test.

Summary questions

1 Put these words into order. They should be in the order that you might use them in an investigation.

design; prediction; conclusion; method; repeat; controls; graph; results; table; improve; safety; hypothesis

2 a How would you tell the difference between an opinion that was scientific and a prejudiced opinion?

b Suppose you were investigating the amount of gas produced in a reaction. Would you choose to investigate a categoric or a continuous variable? Explain why.

3 You might have seen that marble statues weather badly where there is air pollution. You want to find out why.

a You know that sulfur dioxide in the air forms an acid. How could this knowledge help you to make a prediction about the effect of sulfur dioxide on marble statues?

b Make a prediction about the effect of sulfur dioxide on marble statues.

c What experiment could you do to test your prediction?

d Suppose you are not able to carry out an experiment. How else could you test your prediction?

4 a What do you understand by a 'fair test'?

b Suppose you were carrying out an investigation into what effect diluting acid had on its pH. You would need to carry out a trial. Describe what a trial would tell you about how to plan your method.

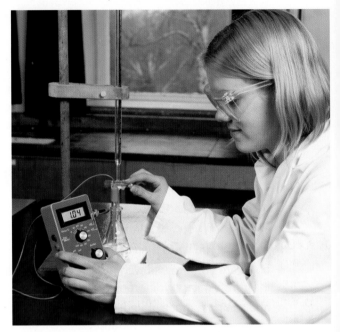

c How could you decide if your results were reliable?

d It is possible to calculate the effect of dilution on the pH of an acid. How could you use this to check on the accuracy of your results?

5 Suppose you were watching a friend carry out an investigation using the equipment shown on page 13. You have to mark your friend on how accurately he is making his measurements. Make a list of points that you would be looking for.

6 a How do you decide on the range of a set of data?

b How do you calculate the mean?

c When should you use a bar chart?

d When should you use a line graph?

7 a What should happen to anomalous results?

b What does a line of best fit allow you to do?

c When making a conclusion, what must you take into consideration?

d How can you check on the repeatability and reproducibility of your results?

8 a Why is it important when reporting science to 'tell the truth, the whole truth and nothing but the truth'?

b Why might some people be tempted not to be completely fair when reporting their opinions on scientific data?

9 a 'Science can advance technology and technology can advance science.' What do you think is meant by this statement?

b Who answers the questions that start with 'Should we … '?

10 Glass has been used for windows in buildings for a long time and is increasingly being used for structural parts as well. It is important therefore to be able to find out the strength of glass. One measure of this is the force that can be applied to glass before it breaks. Glass bends under pressure. Laminated glass is in three layers, glass on the outside sandwiching a polymer layer. This strengthens the glass.

An experiment was carried out to find out how far laminated glass would bend. The glass was supported on two wooden blocks and a load line drawn halfway between the blocks. A load was then placed on this load line and the amount of bend in the glass was measured. The load was gradually increased. Another plate of glass was then used for a second set of results.

Line load (kN/m) with 2–sided support

Apply load   Line load W

The results of the investigation are in the table.

Line load added (kN/m)	Bending Test 1 (mm)	Bending Test 2 (mm)
1	18	20
2	37	39
3	55	57
4	74	76
5	92	98

a What was the prediction for this test?

b What was the independent variable?

c What was the dependent variable?

d Suggest a control variable that should have been used.

e Is there any evidence of a systematic error in this investigation? Explain your answer.

f Is there any evidence of a random error? Explain your answer.

g How could the investigation have its accuracy improved?

h Was the precision of the bending measurement satisfactory? Provide some evidence for your answer from the data in the table.

i What is the mean for the results at a line load of 5 kN/m?

j Draw a graph of the results for the first test.

k Draw a line of best fit.

l Describe the pattern in these results.

m What conclusion can you reach?

n How might you develop this technique to show the effect of the thickness of the polymer on the breaking point of the glass?

o How might this information be used by architects wanting to protect buildings?

C1 1.1 Atoms, elements and compounds

Learning objectives

- What are elements made of?
- How do we represent atoms and elements?
- What is the basic structure of an atom?

Figure 1 An element contains only **one** type of atom – in this case bromine

Look at the things around you and the substances that they are made from. You will find wood, metal, plastic, glass ... the list is almost endless. Look further and the number of different substances is mind-boggling.

All substances are made of **atoms**. There are about 100 different types of atom found naturally on Earth. These can combine in a huge variety of ways. This gives us all those different substances.

Some substances are made up of only one type of atom. We call these substances elements. As there are only about 100 different types of atom, there are only about 100 different elements.

> **a** How many different types of atom are there?
> **b** Why can you make millions of different substances from these different types of atom?

Elements can have very different properties. Elements such as silver, copper and gold are shiny **solids**. Other elements such as oxygen, nitrogen and chlorine are **gases**.

Atoms have their own symbols

The name we use for an element depends on the language being spoken. For example, sulfur is called *Schwefel* in German and *azufre* in Spanish! However, a lot of scientific work is international. So it is important that we have symbols for elements that everyone can understand. You can see these symbols in the **periodic table**.

Group numbers

| Group | 1 | 2 | | | | | | | | | | | 3 | 4 | 5 | 6 | 7 | 0 |

H 1 Hydrogen

| **Li** 3 Lithium | **Be** 4 Beryllium | | | | | | | | | | | **B** 5 Boron | **C** 6 Carbon | **N** 7 Nitrogen | **O** 8 Oxygen | **F** 9 Fluorine | **Ne** 10 Neon |

He 2 Helium

| **Na** 11 Sodium | **Mg** 12 Magnesium | | | | | | | | | | | **Al** 13 Aluminium | **Si** 14 Silicon | **P** 15 Phosphorus | **S** 16 Sulfur | **Cl** 17 Chlorine | **Ar** 18 Argon |

| **K** 19 Potassium | **Ca** 20 Calcium | **Sc** 21 Scandium | **Ti** 22 Titanium | **V** 23 Vanadium | **Cr** 24 Chromium | **Mn** 25 Manganese | **Fe** 26 Iron | **Co** 27 Cobalt | **Ni** 28 Nickel | **Cu** 29 Copper | **Zn** 30 Zinc | **Ga** 31 Gallium | **Ge** 32 Germanium | **As** 33 Arsenic | **Se** 34 Selenium | **Br** 35 Bromine | **Kr** 36 Krypton |

| **Rb** 37 Rubidium | **Sr** 38 Strontium | **Y** 39 Yttrium | **Zr** 40 Zirconium | **Nb** 41 Niobium | **Mo** 42 Molybdenum | **Tc** 43 Technetium | **Ru** 44 Ruthenium | **Rh** 45 Rhodium | **Pd** 46 Palladium | **Ag** 47 Silver | **Cd** 48 Cadmium | **In** 49 Indium | **Sn** 50 Tin | **Sb** 51 Antimony | **Te** 52 Tellurium | **I** 53 Iodine | **Xe** 54 Xenon |

| **Cs** 55 Caesium | **Ba** 56 Barium | Lanthanum see below | **Hf** 72 Hafnium | **Ta** 73 Tantalum | **W** 74 Tungsten | **Re** 75 Rhenium | **Os** 76 Osmium | **Ir** 77 Iridium | **Pt** 78 Platinum | **Au** 79 Gold | **Hg** 80 Mercury | **Tl** 81 Thallium | **Pb** 82 Lead | **Bi** 83 Bismuth | **Po** 84 Polonium | **At** 85 Astatine | **Rn** 86 Radon |

| **Fr** 87 Francium | **Ra** 88 Radium | Actinium see below | | | | | | | | | | | | | | | |

The transition metals

The alkali metals · The alkaline earth metals · The halogens · The noble gases

Lanthanides

| **La** 57 Lanthanum | **Ce** 58 Cerium | **Pr** 59 Praseodymium | **Nd** 60 Neodymium | **Pm** 61 Promethium | **Sm** 62 Samarium | **Eu** 63 Europium | **Gd** 64 Gadolinium | **Tb** 65 Terbium | **Dy** 66 Dysprosium | **Ho** 67 Holmium | **Er** 68 Erbium | **Tm** 69 Thulium | **Yb** 70 Ytterbium | **Lu** 71 Lutetium |

Actinides

| **Ac** 89 Actinium | **Th** 90 Thorium | **Pa** 91 Protactinium | **U** 92 Uranium | **Np** 93 Neptunium | **Pu** 94 Plutonium | **Am** 95 Americium | **Cm** 96 Curium | **Bk** 97 Berkelium | **Cf** 98 Californium | **Es** 99 Einsteinium | **Fm** 100 Fermium | **Md** 101 Mendelevium | **No** 102 Nobelium | **Lr** 103 Lawrencium |

Figure 2 The periodic table shows the symbols for the elements

The symbols in the periodic table represent atoms. For example, O represents an atom of oxygen; Na represents an atom of sodium. The elements in the table are arranged in columns, called **groups**. Each group contains elements with similar chemical properties. The 'staircase' drawn in bold is the dividing line between metals and non-metals. The elements to the left of the line are metals. Those on the right of the line are non-metals.

c   Why is it useful to have symbols for atoms of different elements?
d   Sort these elements into metals and non-metals: phosphorus (P), barium (Ba), vanadium (V), mercury (Hg) and krypton (Kr).

Atoms, elements and compounds

Most of the substances we come across are not pure elements. They are made up of different types of atom joined together. These are called **compounds**. Chemical bonds hold the atoms tightly together in compounds. Some compounds are made from just two types of atom (e.g. water, made from hydrogen and oxygen). Other compounds consist of more different types of atom.

An atom is made up of a tiny central **nucleus** with **electrons** around it.

Electrons

Nucleus

Figure 3 Each atom consists of a small nucleus surrounded by electrons

links

For more information on the periodic table, see C3 1.2 The modern periodic table.

Did you know ... ?

Only 92 elements occur naturally on Earth. The other heavier elements in the periodic table have to be made artificially and might only exist for fractions of a second before they decay into other, lighter elements.

links

For more information on what is inside an atom, see C1 1.2 Atomic structure and 1.3 The arrangement of electrons in atoms.

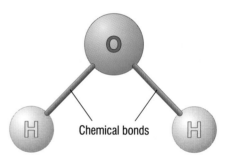

Figure 4 A grouping of two or more atoms bonded together is called a **molecule**. Chemical bonds hold the hydrogen and oxygen atoms together in the water molecule. Water is an example of a compound.

Summary questions

1   Copy and complete using the words below:

atoms   bonds   molecule   compounds

All elements are made up of .... When two or more atoms join together a .... is formed. The atoms in elements and .... are held tightly to each other by chemical ....

2   Explain why when we mix two elements together we can often separate them again quite easily. However, when two elements are chemically combined in a compound, they can be very difficult to separate.

3   Draw diagrams to explain the difference between an element and a compound. Use a hydrogen molecule (H_2) and a hydrogen chloride molecule (HCl) to help explain.

4   Draw a labelled diagram to show the basic structure of an atom.

Key points

• All substances are made up of atoms.

• Elements contain only one type of atom.

• Compounds contain more than one type of atom.

• An atom has a tiny nucleus in its centre, surrounded by electrons.

C1 1.2 Atomic structure

Learning objectives

- What is the charge on a proton, a neutron and an electron?
- What can we say about the number of protons in an atom compared with its number of electrons?
- What is the 'atomic number' and 'mass number' of an atom?
- How are atoms arranged in the periodic table?

In the middle of an atom there is a very small nucleus. This contains two types of particles, which we call **protons** and **neutrons**. A third type of particle orbits the nucleus. We call these really tiny particles electrons.

Any atom has the same number of electrons orbiting its nucleus as it has protons in its nucleus.

Protons have a positive charge. Neutrons have no charge – they are neutral. So the nucleus itself has an overall positive charge.

The electrons orbiting the nucleus are negatively charged. The relative charge on a proton is +1 and the relative charge on an electron is −1.

Because any atom contains equal numbers of protons and electrons, the positive and negative charges cancel out. So there is no overall charge on any atom. Its charge is zero. For example, a carbon atom is neutral. It has 6 protons, so we know it must have 6 electrons.

   a What are the names of the three particles that make up an atom?
   b An oxygen atom has 8 protons – how many electrons does it have?

Did you know …?

In 1808, a chemist called John Dalton published a theory of atoms. It explained how atoms joined together to form new substances (compounds). Not everyone liked his theory though – one person wrote 'Atoms are round bits of wood invented by Mr Dalton!'

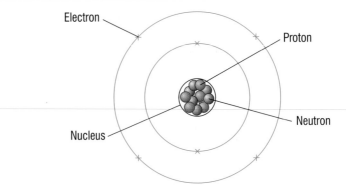

Figure 1 Understanding the structure of an atom gives us important clues to the way chemicals react together

Type of subatomic particle	Relative charge
Proton	+1
Neutron	0
Electron	−1

To help you remember the charge on the subatomic particles:

- **P**rotons are **P**ositive;
- **Neutr**ons are **Neutr**al;
- so that means Electrons must be Negative!

Atomic number and the periodic table

All the atoms of a particular element have the same number of protons. For example, hydrogen has 1 proton in its nucleus, carbon has 6 protons in its nucleus and sodium has 11 protons in its nucleus.

We call the **number of protons** in each atom of an element its **atomic number**.

links

For more information on the structure of atoms, see C2 3.1 The mass of atoms.

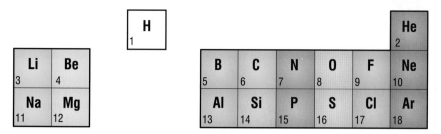

Figure 2 The elements in the periodic table are arranged in order of their atomic number. (As atoms are neutral, this is also the same order as their number of electrons.)

The elements in the periodic table are arranged in order of their atomic number (number of protons). If you are told that the atomic number of an element is 8, you can identify it using the periodic table. It will be the 8th element listed. In this case it is oxygen.

   c What is the 14th element in the periodic table?

You read the periodic table from left to right, and from the top down – just like reading a page of writing.

   d Look at the elements in the last group of the abbreviated periodic table in Figure 2. What pattern do you notice about the number of protons going from helium to neon to argon?

Mass number

The **number of protons plus neutrons** in the nucleus of an atom is called its **mass number**.

- So, if an atom has 4 protons and 5 neutrons, its mass number will be 4 + 5 = **9**.
- Given the atomic number and mass number, we can work out how many protons, electrons and neutrons are in an atom. For example, an argon atom has an atomic number of 18 and a mass number of 40.

  Its atomic number is 18 so it has **18 protons**. Remember that atoms have an equal number of protons and electrons. So argon also has **18 electrons**. The mass number is 40, so we know that:

  18 (the number of protons) + the number of neutrons = 40

  Therefore argon must have **22 neutrons** (as 18 + 22 = 40).

  We can summarise the last part of the calculation as:

  number of neutrons = mass number – atomic number

Summary questions

1 Copy and complete using the words below:

electrons   atomic   negative   neutrons

In the nucleus of atoms there are protons and .... Around the nucleus there are .... which have a .... charge. In the periodic table, atoms are arranged in order of their .... number.

2 Atoms are always neutral. Explain why.

3 How many protons, electrons and neutrons do the following atoms contain?

   a A nitrogen atom whose atomic number is 7 and its mass number is 14.

   b A chlorine atom whose atomic number is 17 and its mass number is 35.

AQA *Examiner's tip*

In an atom, the number of protons is always equal to the number of electrons. You can find out the number of protons and electrons in an atom by looking up its atomic number in the periodic table.

links

For more information on the patterns in the periodic table, see C1 1.3 The arrangement of electrons in atoms.

Key points

- Atoms are made of protons, neutrons and electrons.

- Protons and electrons have equal and opposite electric charges. Protons are positively charged, and electrons are negatively charged.

- Neutrons have no electric charge. They are neutral.

- Atomic number = number of protons (= number of electrons) Mass number = number of protons + neutrons

- Atoms are arranged in the periodic table in order of their atomic number.

The arrangement of electrons in atoms

C1 1.3

Learning objectives

- How are the electrons arranged inside an atom?

- How is the number of electrons in the highest energy level of an atom related to its group in the periodic table?

- How is the number of electrons in the highest energy level of an atom related to its chemical properties?

- Why are the atoms of Group 0 elements so unreactive?

One model of the atom which we use has electrons arranged around the nucleus in **shells**, rather like the layers of an onion. Each shell represents a different **energy level**. The lowest energy level is shown by the shell which is nearest to the nucleus. The electrons in an atom occupy the lowest available energy level (the shell closest to the nucleus).

  a Where are the electrons in an atom?
  b Which shell represents the lowest energy level in an atom?

Electron shell diagrams

We can draw diagrams to show the arrangement of electrons in an atom. A carbon atom has 6 protons, which means it has 6 electrons. Figure 1 shows how we represent an atom of carbon.

An energy level (or shell) can only hold a certain number of electrons.

- The first, and lowest, energy level holds 2 electrons.
- The second energy level can hold up to 8 electrons.
- Once there are 8 electrons in the third energy level, the fourth begins to fill up, and so on.

To save drawing atoms all the time, we can write down the numbers of electrons in each energy level. This is called the **electronic structure**. For example, the carbon atom in Figure 1 has an electronic structure of 2,4.

A silicon atom with 14 electrons has the electronic structure 2,8,4. This represents 2 electrons in the first, and lowest, energy level, then 8 in the next energy level. There are 4 in the highest energy level (its outermost shell).

The best way to understand these arrangements is to look at some examples.

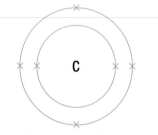

Figure 1 A simple way of representing the arrangement of electrons in the energy levels (shells) of a carbon atom

AQA *Examiner's tip*

Make sure that you can draw the electronic structure of the atoms for all of the first 20 elements. You will always be given their atomic number or their position in the periodic table (which tells you the number of electrons) – so you don't have to memorise these numbers.

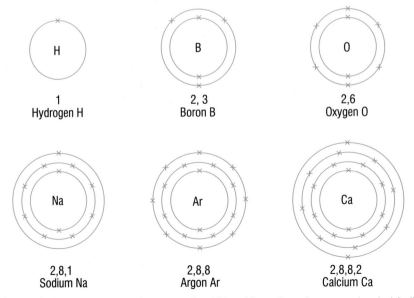

1 Hydrogen H	2, 3 Boron B	2,6 Oxygen O
2,8,1 Sodium Na	2,8,8 Argon Ar	2,8,8,2 Calcium Ca

Figure 2 Once you know the pattern, you should be able to draw the energy levels (shells) and electrons in any of the first 20 atoms (given their atomic number)

c How many electrons can the first energy level hold?

d What is the electronic structure of sulfur (whose atoms contain 16 electrons)?

Electrons and the periodic table

Look at the elements in any one of the main groups of the periodic table. Their atoms will all have the same number of electrons in their highest energy level. These electrons are often called the outer electrons because they are in the outermost shell. Therefore, all the elements in Group 1 have one electron in their highest energy level.

Demonstration

Properties of the Group 1 elements

Your teacher will show you the Group 1 elements lithium, sodium and potassium. The elements in this group are called the **alkali metals**. Make sure you wear eye protection for all the demonstrations.

● In what ways are the elements similar?

● Watch their reactions with water and comment on the similarities.

● You might also be shown their reactions with oxygen.

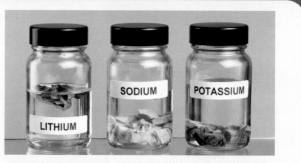

Figure 3 The Group 1 metals are all reactive metals, stored under oil

The chemical properties of an element depend on how many electrons it has. The way an element reacts is determined by the number of electrons in its highest energy level (or outermost shell). So as the elements in a particular group all have the same number of electrons in their highest energy level, they all react in a similar way.

For example:

lithium   + water → lithium hydroxide   + hydrogen
sodium   + water → sodium hydroxide   + hydrogen
potassium + water → potassium hydroxide + hydrogen

The elements in Group 0 of the periodic table are called the noble gases because they are unreactive. Their atoms have a very stable arrangement of electrons. They all have 8 electrons in their outermost shell, except for helium, which has only 2 electrons.

Summary questions

1 Copy and complete using the words below:

electrons energy group nucleus shells

The electrons in an atom are arranged around the .... in .... (energy levels). The electrons further away from the nucleus have more .... than those close to the nucleus. All elements in the same .... of the periodic table have the same number of .... in their outermost shell.

2 Using the periodic table, draw the arrangement of electrons in the following atoms and label each one with its electronic structure.

  a Li   **b** B   **c** P   **d** Ar

3 What is special about the electronic structure of neon and argon?

Key points

● The electrons in an atom are arranged in energy levels or shells.

● Atoms with the same number of electrons in their outermost shell belong in the same group of the periodic table.

● The number of electrons in the outermost shell of an element's atoms determines the way that element reacts.

● The atoms of the unreactive noble gases (in Group 0) all have very stable arrangements of electrons.

C1 1.4

Forming bonds

Learning objectives

- How do metals and non-metals bond to each other?
- How do non-metals bond to each other?
- How do we write the formula of a compound?

AQA Examiner's tip

When counting atoms, think of each symbol as a single atom and the formula of each ion as a single ion. Small numbers in a chemical formula only multiply the symbol they follow. Brackets are needed when there is more than one atom in the ion being multiplied. For example, a hydroxide ion has the formula OH^-. So calcium hydroxide, in which Ca^{2+} and OH^- combine, has the formula $Ca(OH)_2$.

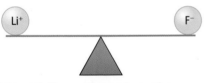

Figure 2 The positive and negative charge on the ions in a compound balance each other, making the total charge zero

It is useful for us to know how atoms bond to each other in different substances. It helps us to predict and explain their properties.

How Science Works

Predicting what material to use

A team of research chemists and material scientists are working to make a new compound for the latest surfboard. Knowing about chemical bonding will make the process of designing a new compound a lot quicker.

Figure 1 Surfboards have to be very strong and have a relatively low density

The substances used to make a surfboard have to be very strong (to withstand large forces) and have a relatively low density (to float on water). Chemists help design materials with suitable properties. They will know before they start which combinations of atoms might prove useful to investigate.

Sometimes atoms react together by **transferring** electrons to form chemical bonds. This happens when metals react with non-metals. If the reacting atoms are all non-metals, then the atoms **share** electrons to form chemical bonds.

Forming ions

When a metal bonds with a non-metal, the metal atom gives one or more electrons to the non-metal atom. Both atoms become charged particles called **ions**.

- Metal atoms form positively charged ions (+).
- Non-metal atoms form negatively charged ions (−).

Opposite charges attract each other. There are strong attractions between the positive and negative ions in a compound of a metal and non-metal. These strong forces of attraction are the chemical bonds that form. They are called **ionic bonds**.

To see how ions are formed we can look at an example. Lithium metal will react with the non-metal fluorine. They make the compound lithium fluoride. Lithium atoms have 3 electrons, each negatively charged. As all atoms are neutral, we know it also has 3 positive protons in its nucleus. The charges on the negative electrons are balanced by the positive protons.

When lithium reacts with fluorine it loses 1 electron. This leaves it with only 2 electrons. However, there are still 3 protons in the nucleus. Therefore the lithium ion carries a 1+ charge.	The electron lost from lithium is accepted by a fluorine atom. A fluorine atom has 9 electrons and 9 protons, making the atom neutral. However, with the extra electron from lithium, it has an extra 1− charge:

3 protons = 3+
2 electrons = 2−
Charge on ion = 1+

We show the formula of a lithium ion as **Li⁺**.

9 protons = 9+
10 electrons = 10−
Charge on ion = 1−

We show the formula of a fluoride ion as **F⁻**.

Notice the spelling – we have a fluor**ine** atom which turns into a negatively charged fluor**ide** ion.

In compounds between metals and non-metals, the charges on the ions always cancel each other out. This means that their compounds have no overall charge. So the formula of lithium fluoride is written as **LiF**.

> **a** Potassium (K) is a metal. It loses one electron when it forms an ion. What is the formula of a potassium ion?

Forming molecules

Non-metal atoms bond to each other in a different way. The outermost shells of their atoms overlap and they share electrons. Each pair of shared electrons forms a chemical bond between the atoms. These are called **covalent bonds**. No ions are formed. They form molecules, such as hydrogen sulfide, H_2S, and methane, CH_4 (see Figure 3).

> **b** What do we call the bonds between nitrogen and hydrogen atoms in an ammonia molecule, NH_3?

Chemical formulae

The chemical formula of an ionic compound tells us the ratio of each type of ion in the compound. We use a ratio because when ions bond together they form structures made of many millions of ions. The ratio depends on the charge on each ion. The charges must cancel each other out.

An example is magnesium chloride. Magnesium forms Mg^{2+} ions and chlorine forms Cl^- ions. So the formula of magnesium chloride is $MgCl_2$. We have 2 chloride ions for every one magnesium ion in the compound (see Figure 4).

In covalent molecules we can just count the number of each type of atom in a molecule to get its formula. Figure 3 shows two examples.

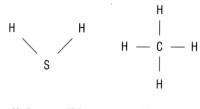

Hydrogen sulfide   Methane

Figure 3 There are strong covalent bonds between the non-metal atoms in each of these molecules. These are shown as lines between each atom or between the symbols of each atom in the molecule (H_2S and CH_4).

Figure 4 The 2+ positive charge on the magnesium ion balances the two 1− negative charges on the chloride ions in magnesium chloride ($MgCl_2$)

Key points

● When atoms from different elements react together they make compounds. The formula of a compound shows the number and type of atoms that have bonded together to make that compound.

● When metals react with non-metals, charged particles called ions are formed.

● Metal atoms form positively charged ions. Non-metal atoms form negatively charged ions. These oppositely charged ions attract each other in ionic bonding.

● Atoms of non-metals bond to each other by sharing electrons. This is called covalent bonding.

Summary questions

1 Copy and complete using the words below:

covalent   lose   gain   ionic   negative   attract   share   positive

Metal atoms form .... ions because they .... one or more electrons when they combine with non-metals. Non-metal atoms .... electrons in the reaction, forming .... ions. The oppositely charged ions .... each other. This is called .... bonding.

When non-metals combine with each other, they form .... bonds. Their atoms .... electrons.

2 Sodium (Na) atoms lose one electron when they combine with fluorine (F). Each fluorine atom gains one electron in the reaction.
  a What is the name of the compound formed when sodium reacts with fluorine?
  b Write down the formula of a sodium ion and a fluoride ion.
  c What is the formula of the compound made when sodium reacts with fluorine.

C1 1.5 Chemical equations ⓚ

Learning objectives

- What happens to the atoms in a chemical reaction?

- How does the mass of reactants compare with the mass of products in a chemical reaction?

- How can we write balanced symbol equations to represent reactions? [H]

Chemical equations show the **reactants** (the substances we start with) and the **products** (the new substances made) of a reaction.

We can represent the test for hydrogen gas using a **word equation**:

$$\text{hydrogen} + \text{oxygen} \rightarrow \text{water}$$
$$\text{(reactants)} \qquad \text{(product)}$$

a State what happens in a positive test for hydrogen gas.

In chemical reactions the atoms get rearranged. You can think of them 'swapping partners'. Now you can investigate what happens to the mass of reactants compared with mass of products in a reaction.

Practical

Investigating the mass of reactants and products

You are given solutions of lead nitrate (toxic) and potassium iodide.

Wearing chemical splashproof eye protection, add a small volume of each solution together in a test tube.

- What do you see happen?

The formula of lead nitrate is $Pb(NO_3)_2$ and potassium iodide is KI.

The precipitate (a solid suspended in the solution) formed in the reaction is lead iodide, PbI_2 (toxic).

- Predict a word equation for the reaction.
- How do you think that the mass of reactants compare with the mass of the products?

Now plan an experiment to test your answer to this question.

Using **symbol equations** helps us to see how much of each substance is reacting. Representing reactions in this way is better than using word equations, for three reasons.

- Word equations are only useful if everyone who reads them speaks the same language.
- Word equations do not tell us how much of each substance is involved in the reaction.
- Word equations can get very complicated when lots of chemicals are involved.

For example, calcium carbonate decomposes (breaks down) on heating. We can show the reaction using a symbol equation like this:

$$CaCO_3 \rightarrow CaO + CO_2$$

This equation is **balanced** – there is the same number of each type of atom on both sides of the equation. This is very important, because atoms cannot be created or destroyed in a chemical reaction. This also means that:

The total mass of the products formed in a reaction is equal to the total mass of the reactants.

b Name the reactant and products in the decomposition of calcium carbonate.

We can check if an equation is balanced by counting the number of each type of atom on either side of the equation. If the numbers are equal, then the equation is balanced.

⫘ links

For more information on the decomposition of calcium carbonate, see C1 2.1 Limestone and its uses.

Maths skills

Look at the chemical equation on the previous page. We can work out the mass of $CaCO_3$, CaO or CO_2 given the masses of the other two compounds.

Because the total mass of the products formed in a reaction is equal to the total mass of the reactants we can write:

$$CaCO_3 \rightarrow CaO + CO_2$$
$$Mass = \quad a \quad = \quad b \quad + \quad c$$

So if the mass of CaO formed is 2.8 g (b above) and the mass of CO_2 is 2.2 g (c above); the mass of $CaCO_3$

(a) that we start with must be 2.8 + 2.2 (b + c) which equals **5.0 g**.

Rearranging the equation for a, b and c we get $a - c = b$.

So if the reaction started with 100 tonnes of $CaCO_3$ (a) and it gave off 44 tonnes of CO_2 (c),

Then the mass of CaO (b) made is 100 − 44 (a − c) = **56 tonnes**.

Higher

Making an equation balance

In the case of hydrogen reacting with oxygen it is not so easy to balance the equation. First of all we write the formula of each reactant and product:

$$H_2 + O_2 \rightarrow H_2O$$

Counting the atoms on either side of the equation we see that we have:

Reactants
2 H atoms, 2 O atoms

Products
2 H atoms, 1 O atom

So we need another oxygen atom on the product side of the equation. We can't simply change the formula of H_2O to H_2O_2. (H_2O_2 – hydrogen peroxide is a bleaching agent which is certainly not suitable to drink!) But we can have **2 water molecules** in the reaction – this is shown in a symbol equation as:

$$H_2 + O_2 \rightarrow \mathbf{2H_2O}$$

Counting the atoms on either side of the equation again we get:

Reactants
2 H atoms, 2 O atoms

Products
4 H atoms, 2 O atom

Although the oxygen atoms are balanced, we now need two more hydrogen atoms on the reactant side. We do this by putting 2 in front of H_2:

$$\mathbf{2H_2 + O_2 \rightarrow 2H_2O}$$

Now we have:

Reactants
4 H atoms, 2 O atoms

Products
4 H atoms, 2 O atom

.... and the equation is balanced.

c Balance the following equation: $H_2 + Cl_2 \rightarrow HCl$

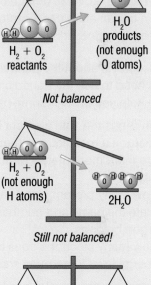

$H_2 + O_2$ reactants

H_2O products (not enough O atoms)

Not balanced

$H_2 + O_2$ (not enough H atoms)

$2H_2O$

Still not balanced!

$2H_2 + O_2$

$2H_2O$

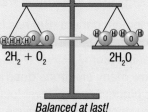

Balanced at last!

Summary questions

1 Why must all symbol equations be balanced?

2 **a** A mass of 8.4 g of magnesium carbonate ($MgCO_3$) completely decomposes when it is heated. It made 4.0 g of magnesium oxide (MgO). What is the total mass of carbon dioxide (CO_2) produced in this reaction?

   b Write a word equation to show the reaction in part **a**.

3 Balance these symbol equations:
   a $Ca + O_2 \rightarrow CaO$ **b** $Al + O_2 \rightarrow Al_2O_3$ **c** $Na + H_2O \rightarrow NaOH + H_2$ [H]

Key points

● As no new atoms are ever created or destroyed in a chemical reaction:
The total mass of reactants = the total mass of products

● There is the same number of each type of atom on each side of a balanced symbol equation.

Summary questions ⓚ

1 a What is the difference in the definitions of an element and a compound?

b The chemical formula of ethanol is written as C_2H_5OH.
  i How many atoms of hydrogen are there in an ethanol molecule?
  ii How many different elements are there in ethanol?
  iii What is the total number of atoms in an ethanol molecule?

2 a Draw a table to show the relative charge on protons, neutrons and electrons.

b In which part of an atom do we find:
  i protons
  ii neutrons
  iii electrons.

c i What is the overall charge on any atom?
  ii A nitrogen atom has 7 protons. How many electrons does it have?

3 This question is about the periodic table of elements. You will need to use the periodic table at the back of this book to help you answer some parts of the question.

a Argon (Ar) is the 18th element in the periodic table.
  i Is argon a metal or a non-metal?
  ii Are there more metals or non-metals in the periodic table?
  iii How many protons does an argon atom contain?
  iv State the name and number of the group to which argon belongs.
  v How many electrons does argon have in its highest energy level (outermost shell)?

b The element barium (Ba) has 56 electrons.
  i How many protons are in the nucleus of each barium atom?
  ii How many electrons does a barium atom have in its highest energy level (outermost shell)? How did you decide on your answer?
  iii Is barium a metal or a non-metal?

4 The diagram below shows the arrangement of electrons in an atom.

a How many protons are in the nucleus of this atom?

b Use the periodic table at the back of this book to give the name and symbol of the element whose atom is shown here.

c This element forms ions with a 1+ charge.
  i What is an ion?
  ii How does the charge on the ion tell us whether the element above is a metal or non-metal?
  iii Describe what happens to the number of electrons when the atom forms a 1+ ion.
  iv Write the chemical formula of the ion.
  v This ion can form compounds with negatively charged ions. What type of bonding will we find in these compounds?

d A compound is formed when this element reacts with chlorine gas.
  i What is the name of the compound formed?
  ii Chloride ions carry a 1− charge. Write the chemical formula of the compound formed.

5 What is the missing number needed to balance the following symbol equations?

a $2Na + Cl_2 \rightarrow \text{....} NaCl$

b $2Zn + O_2 \rightarrow \text{....} ZnO$

c $\text{....} Cr + 3O_2 \rightarrow 2Cr_2O_3$

d $C_3H_8 + \text{....} O_2 \rightarrow 3CO_2 + 4H_2O$ **[H]**

6 Balance the following symbol equations:

a $H_2 + Br_2 \rightarrow HBr$

b $Mg + O_2 \rightarrow MgO$

c $H_2O_2 \rightarrow H_2O + O_2$

d $Li + H_2O \rightarrow LiOH + H_2$

e $NaNO_3 \rightarrow NaNO_2 + O_2$

f $Fe + O_2 \rightarrow Fe_2O_3$ **[H]**

7 When a mixture of iron and sulfur is heated, a compound called iron sulfide is made.

In an experiment 2.8 g of iron made 4.4 g of iron sulfide.

a What mass of sulfur reacted with the 2.8 g of iron?

b Explain how you worked out your answer to part **a**.

AQA Examination-style questions ⓚ

1 Use numbers from the list to complete the table to show the charge on each subatomic particle.

+2   +1   0   −1   −2

Subatomic particle	Charge
electron	
neutron	
proton	

(3)

2 Use the periodic table at the back of your book to help you to answer this question.

a How many protons are in an atom of fluorine? (1)

b How many electrons are in an atom of carbon? (1)

c Complete the electronic structure of aluminium: 2,8, ... (1)

d What is the electronic structure of potassium? (1)

3 Neon is a noble gas.

a What does this tell you about its electronic structure? (1)

b Draw a diagram to show the electronic structure of neon. (2)

4 a Magnesium has the electronic structure 2,8,2. Explain, in terms of its electronic structure, why magnesium is in Group 2 of the periodic table. (1)

b Give **one** way in which the electronic structures of the atoms of Group 2 elements are:
i the same (1)
ii different. (1)

c When magnesium is heated in air it burns with a bright flame and produces magnesium oxide.

Calcium is also in Group 2. Describe what you expect to happen and what would be produced when calcium is heated in air. (2)

5 Sodium reacts with water to produce sodium hydroxide and hydrogen.

The word equation for this reaction is:

sodium + water → sodium hydroxide + hydrogen

a Name one substance in this equation that is:
i an element (1)
ii a compound (1)
iii has ionic bonds (1)
iv has covalent bonds (1)

b If 2.3 g of sodium reacted with 1.8 g of water, what would be the total mass of sodium hydroxide and hydrogen produced?
Explain your answer. (2)

c Balance the symbol equation for this reaction.

.... Na + ... H_2O → .... $NaOH$ + H_2 [H] (1)

d Lithium is in the same group of the periodic table as sodium.
i Write a word equation for the reaction of lithium with water. (1)
ii What is the formula of lithium hydroxide? (1)
iii How many atoms are shown in the formula of lithium hydroxide you have written? (1)

C1 2.1 Limestone and its uses

Learning objectives

- What are the uses of limestone?
- What happens when we heat limestone?

Figure 1 St Paul's Cathedral in London is built from limestone blocks

??? Did you know ... ?

Chalk is a form of limestone. It was formed millions of years ago from the skeletal remains of tiny sea plants called coccoliths. They were deposited on the seabed between 65 and 130 million years ago. It has been estimated that it took almost 100 000 years to lay down each metre of chalk in a cliff face.

∞ links

For information on the formulae of compounds made up of ions, look back at C1 1.4 Forming bonds.

Uses of limestone Ⓚ

Limestone is a rock that is made mainly of **calcium carbonate**. Some types of limestone were formed from the remains of tiny animals and plants that lived in the sea millions of years ago. We dig limestone out of the ground in quarries all around the world. It has many uses, including its use as a building material.

Many important buildings around the world are made of limestone. We can cut and shape the stone taken from the ground into blocks. These can be placed one on top of the other, like bricks in a wall. We have used limestone in this way to make buildings for hundreds of years.

Powdered limestone can also be heated with powdered clay to make **cement**. When we mix cement powder with water, sand and crushed rock, a slow chemical reaction takes place. The reaction produces a hard, stone-like building material called **concrete**.

Figure 2 These white cliffs are made of chalk. This is one type of limestone, formed from the shells of tiny sea plants.

Figure 3 This building contains plenty of concrete which is made from limestone

a What is the main compound found in limestone?
b How do we use limestone to make buildings?

Heating limestone

The chemical formula for calcium carbonate is **$CaCO_3$**. It is made up of calcium ions, Ca^{2+}, and carbonate ions, CO_3^{2-}. The 2+ and 2− charges tell us that there are the same number of calcium ions and carbonate ions in calcium carbonate. Remember that the charges on the ions cancel out in compounds.

When we heat limestone strongly, the calcium carbonate breaks down to form calcium oxide. Carbon dioxide is also produced in this reaction. Breaking down a chemical by heating is called **thermal decomposition**.

We can show the thermal decomposition reaction using the following equations:

Word equation: $$\text{calcium carbonate} \xrightarrow{\text{heat}} \text{calcium oxide} + \text{carbon dioxide}$$

Balanced symbol equation: $$CaCO_3 \rightarrow CaO + CO_2$$

The calcium oxide made is also a very useful substance in the building and farming industries.

Practical

Thermal decomposition

In this experiment you can carry out the reaction that takes place in a lime kiln.

Safety: Make sure the rubber tube is tightly secured to the gas tap and the Bunsen burner before starting the experiment. Do not overstretch the tubing. Do not touch the decomposed carbonate as it is corrosive. Wash your hands if you get any chemicals on them. Wear eye protection.

Place a limestone chip on a tripod and gauze. Using a roaring flame, hold the base of the Bunsen burner and heat a limestone chip strongly from the side. It is best if the tip of the blue cone of the flame heats the limestone directly. You will see signs of a reaction happening on the surface of the limestone.

- What do you see happen as the limestone is heated strongly?

A rotary lime kiln

To make lots of calcium oxide this reaction is done in a furnace called a **lime kiln**. We fill the kiln with crushed limestone and heat it strongly using a supply of hot air. Calcium oxide comes out of the bottom of the kiln. Waste gases, including the carbon dioxide made, leave the kiln at the top.

Calcium oxide is often produced in a **rotary kiln**, where the limestone is heated in a rotating drum. This makes sure that the limestone is thoroughly mixed with the stream of hot air.
This helps the calcium carbonate to decompose completely.

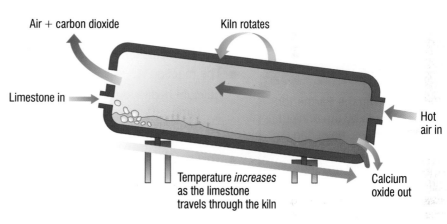

Figure 4 Calcium oxide is produced in a rotary lime kiln

∞ **links**

For more information on the uses of calcium oxide, see C1 2.3 The 'limestone reaction cycle'.

Summary questions

1 Copy and complete using the words below:

building   calcium   cement   concrete

Limestone is mostly made of .... carbonate (whose chemical formula is $CaCO_3$). As well as making blocks of building material, limestone can be used to produce .... and .... that are also used in the .... industry.

2 Produce a poster or PowerPoint presentation to show how limestone is used in building.

3 The stone roof of a building is supported by columns made of limestone. Why might this be unsafe after a fire in the building? Explain the chemical reaction involved in weakening the structure.

Key points

- Limestone is made mainly of calcium carbonate.

- Limestone is widely used in the building industry.

- The calcium carbonate in limestone breaks down when we heat it strongly to make calcium oxide and carbon dioxide. The reaction is called thermal decomposition.

C1 2.2 | Reactions of carbonates

Learning objectives

- Do other carbonates behave in the same way as calcium carbonate?

- What happens when dilute acid is added to a carbonate?

- What is the test for carbon dioxide gas?

Buildings and statues made of limestone suffer badly from damage by acid rain. You might have noticed statues where the fine features have been lost. Limestone is mostly calcium carbonate, which reacts with acid. A gas is given off in the reaction.

Testing for carbon dioxide

You can use a simple test to find out if the gas given off is carbon dioxide. Carbon dioxide turns **limewater** solution cloudy. The test works as follows:

- Limewater is a solution of calcium hydroxide. It is alkaline.

- Carbon dioxide is a weakly acidic gas so it reacts with the alkaline limewater.

Figure 1 Limestone is attacked and damaged by acids

- In this reaction tiny solid particles of insoluble calcium carbonate are formed as a precipitate.

- The reaction is:

calcium hydroxide + carbon dioxide → calcium carbonate + water
(limewater)　　　　　　　　　　　　　(an insoluble precipitate)

$$Ca(OH)_2 + CO_2 \rightarrow CaCO_3 + H_2O$$

- This precipitate of calcium carbonate makes the limewater turn cloudy. That's because light can no longer pass through the solution with tiny bits of white solid suspended in it.

a What is a precipitate?

Carbonates react with acids to give a salt, water and carbon dioxide. For calcium carbonate the reaction with hydrochloric acid is:

calcium carbonate + hydrochloric acid → calcium chloride + water + carbon dioxide

The balanced symbol equation is:

$$CaCO_3 + 2HCl \rightarrow CaCl_2 + H_2O + CO_2$$

b Write a word equation for the reaction of magnesium carbonate with hydrochloric acid.

?? Did you know … ?

Sculptures from the Parthenon (a temple), built by the ancient Greeks in Athens, have had to be removed and replaced by copies to avoid any more damage from acid pollution from vehicle exhausts.

Figure 2 The Parthenon in Greece

Practical

Acid plus carbonates (k)

Set up the apparatus as shown.

Try the test with some other carbonates, such as those of magnesium, copper, zinc and sodium.

Record your observations.

- What conclusion can you draw?

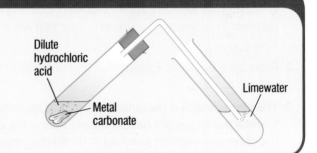

Dilute hydrochloric acid

Limewater

Metal carbonate

Decomposing carbonates (k)

In C1 2.1 we saw that limestone is made up mainly of calcium carbonate. This decomposes when we heat it. The reaction produces calcium oxide and carbon dioxide. Calcium is an element in Group 2 of the periodic table. As we have already seen, the elements in a group tend to behave in the same way. So, does magnesium carbonate also decompose when you heat it? And what about other carbonates too?

c Why might you expect magnesium carbonate to behave in a similar way to calcium carbonate?

Practical

Investigating carbonates

You can investigate the thermal decomposition of carbonates by heating samples in a Bunsen flame. You will have samples of the carbonates listed below.

Powdered carbonate samples: sodium carbonate, potassium carbonate, magnesium carbonate, zinc carbonate, copper carbonate

● What observations might tell you if a sample decomposes when you heat it?
● How could you test any gas given off?

Plan an investigation to find out how easily different carbonates decompose.

● How will you try to make it a fair test?
● How will you make your investigation safe?

Before you start any practical work, your teacher must check your plan.

Safety: It is important to remove the delivery tube from the limewater before you stop heating the carbonate. If you don't, the cold limewater will be 'sucked back' into the hot boiling tube causing it to smash. You must wear eye protection when doing this practical.

Figure 3 Investigating the thermal decomposition of a solid

Investigations like this show that many metal carbonates decompose when they are heated in a Bunsen flame. They form the metal oxide and carbon dioxide – just as calcium carbonate does. Sodium and potassium carbonate do not decompose at the temperature of the Bunsen flame. They need a higher temperature.

Magnesium carbonate decomposes like this:

$$\text{magnesium carbonate} \rightarrow \text{magnesium oxide} + \text{carbon dioxide}$$
$$MgCO_3 \rightarrow MgO + CO_2$$

Summary questions

1 Give a general word equation for:
  a the reaction of a carbonate plus an acid
  b the thermal decomposition of a carbonate.

2 Write a word equation for the reaction of sodium carbonate with dilute hydrochloric acid.

3 The formula of zinc carbonate is $ZnCO_3$.
  a Zinc carbonate decomposes when heated, giving zinc oxide and carbon dioxide. Write the balanced equation for this reaction. **[H]**
  b Write the balanced symbol equation for the reaction of zinc carbonate with dilute hydrochloric acid. **[H]**

Key points

● Carbonates react with dilute acid to form a salt, water and carbon dioxide.

● Limewater turns cloudy in the test for carbon dioxide gas. A precipitate of insoluble calcium carbonate causes the cloudiness.

● Metal carbonates decompose on heating to form the metal oxide and carbon dioxide.

C1 2.3 The 'limestone reaction cycle' ⓚ

Learning objectives

- How can we make calcium hydroxide from calcium oxide?

- Why is calcium hydroxide a useful substance?

- What is the 'limestone reaction cycle'?

Limestone is used very widely as a building material. We can also use it to make other materials for the construction industry.

As we saw in C1 2.1 **calcium oxide** is made when we heat limestone strongly. The calcium carbonate in the limestone undergoes thermal decomposition.

When we add water to calcium oxide it reacts to produce **calcium hydroxide**. This reaction gives out a lot of heat.

$$\text{calcium oxide} + \text{water} \rightarrow \text{calcium hydroxide}$$
$$CaO + H_2O \rightarrow Ca(OH)_2$$

Although it is not very soluble, we can dissolve a little calcium hydroxide in water. After filtering, this produces a colourless solution called limewater. We can use limewater to test for carbon dioxide.

a What substance do we get when calcium oxide reacts with water?

b Describe how we can make limewater from calcium hydroxide.

Practical

Investigating the 'limestone reaction cycle' ⓚ

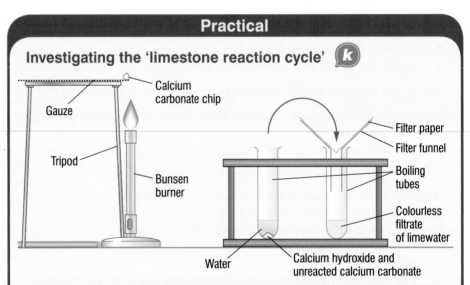

Heat the calcium carbonate chip very strongly, making it glow. Make sure you are wearing eye protection. The greater the area of the chip that glows, the better the rest of the experiment will be. This reaction produces calcium oxide (corrosive). Let the calcium oxide cool down. Then, using tongs, add it to the empty boiling tube.

Then you add a few drops of water to the calcium oxide, one drop at a time. This reaction produces calcium hydroxide.

When you dissolve this calcium hydroxide in more water and filter, it produces limewater.

Carbon dioxide bubbled through the limewater produces calcium carbonate. This turns the solution cloudy.

- The reaction between calcium oxide and water gives out a lot of energy. What do you observe during the reaction?

- Why does bubbling carbon dioxide through limewater make the solution go cloudy?

AQA *Examiner's tip*

Make sure that you know the limestone reaction cycle and the equations for each reaction.

🔗 **links**

For information on the test for carbon dioxide, look back at C1 2.2 Reactions of carbonates.

The reactions in the experiment can be shown on a flow diagram:

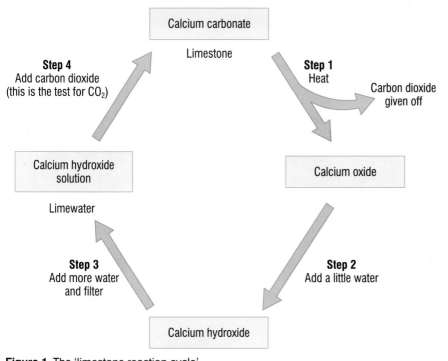

Figure 1 The 'limestone reaction cycle'

The 'limestone reaction cycle'

Neutralising acids

Calcium hydroxide is an alkali. It reacts with acids in a neutralisation reaction. The products of the reaction are a calcium salt and water.

Calcium hydroxide is used by farmers to improve soil that is acidic. Because it is an alkali, it will raise the pH of acidic soil. It is also used to neutralise acidic waste gases in industry before releasing gases into the air.

Summary questions

1 Copy and complete using the words below:

   carbon   limewater   hydroxide   carbonate   water   oxide

   When limestone is heated, the calcium .... in it decomposes to produce calcium .... and .... dioxide gas. If calcium oxide is reacted with water, calcium .... is produced. When we add more .... and filter we make a solution of calcium hydroxide called ....

2 Describe and explain the positive test for carbon dioxide gas. Include a word equation in your answer. (See C1 2.2).

3 a When calcium oxide reacts with water, calcium hydroxide is produced. Write a word equation and a balanced symbol equation to show the reaction.   [H]

   b Calcium hydroxide is an alkali so it reacts with acids.

   i   Give one use of calcium hydroxide that relies on this reaction.

   ii What do we call this type of reaction?

4 Why do we refer to the series of reactions in the practical box on the previous page as the 'limestone reaction cycle'?

Key points

- When water is added to calcium oxide it produces calcium hydroxide.

- Calcium hydroxide is alkaline so it can be used to neutralise acids.

- The reactions of limestone and its products that you need to know are shown in the 'limestone reaction cycle'.

C1 2.4

Cement and concrete

Learning objectives

- How has mortar developed over time?
- How do we make cement?
- What is concrete?
- How can you improve the quality of data collected in an investigation?

Figure 2 The original lime mortar has flaked away from the surface of the Sphinx in Egypt, and many of the stones are now missing

Figure 1 Lime mortar is not suitable for building pools as it will not harden when in contact with water

⚙ How Science Works

Development of lime mortar

About 6000 years ago the Egyptians heated limestone strongly in a fire and then combined it with water. This produced a material that hardened with age. They used this material to plaster the pyramids. Nearly 4000 years later, the Romans mixed calcium hydroxide with sand and water to produce **mortar**.

Mortar holds other building materials together – for example, stone blocks or bricks. It works because the lime in the mortar reacts with carbon dioxide in the air, producing calcium carbonate again. This means that the bricks or stone blocks are effectively held together by rock.

calcium hydroxide + carbon dioxide → calcium carbonate + water
$$Ca(OH)_2 \quad + \quad CO_2 \quad \rightarrow \quad CaCO_3 \quad + \quad H_2O$$

The amount of sand in the mixture is very important. Too little sand and the mortar shrinks as it dries. Too much sand makes it too weak.

Even today, mortar is still used widely as a building material. However, modern mortars, made with cement in place of calcium hydroxide, can be used in a much wider range of ways than lime mortar.

Cement

Although lime mortar holds bricks and stone together very strongly, it does have some disadvantages. For example, lime mortar does not harden very quickly. It will not set at all where water prevents it from reacting with carbon dioxide.

Then people found that heating limestone with clay in a kiln produced cement. Much experimenting led to the invention of Portland cement. This is manufactured from a mixture of limestone, clay and other minerals. They are heated and then ground up into a fine powder.

This type of cement is still in use today. The mortar used to build a modern house is made by mixing Portland cement and sand. This sets when it is mixed thoroughly with water and left for a few days.

a What does lime mortar need in order to set hard?

b Why will lime mortar not set under water?

Concrete ⓚ

Sometimes builders add small stones or crushed rocks, called aggregate, to the mixture of water, cement and sand. When this sets, it forms a hard, rock-like building material called concrete.

This material is very strong. It is especially good at resisting forces which tend to squash or crush it. We can make concrete even stronger by pouring the wet mixture around steel rods or bars and then allowing it to set. This makes reinforced concrete, which is also good at resisting forces that tend to pull it apart.

Figure 3 Portland cement was invented nearly 200 years ago. It is still in use all around the world today.

⚙ Practical

Which mixture makes the strongest concrete?

Try mixing different proportions of cement, gravel and sand, then adding water, to find out how to make the strongest concrete.

● How can you test the concrete's strength?

● How could you improve the quality of the data you collect?

Summary questions

1 Copy and complete using the words below:

mortar concrete clay sand bricks

Cement is made in industry by heating limestone with .... It can be mixed with sand to produce ...., used to hold building materials like .... in place. An even stronger material is made by mixing cement, ... and aggregate to make ....

2 List the different ways in which limestone has been used to build your home or school.

3 Concrete and mortar are commonly used building materials. Evaluate the use of:

a concrete to make a path rather than using mortar

b mortar to bind bricks to each other rather than using concrete.

Key points

● Cement is made by heating limestone with clay in a kiln.

● Mortar is made by mixing cement and sand with water.

● Concrete is made by mixing crushed rocks or small stones called aggregate, cement and sand with water.

Summary questions ⓚ

1 In the process of manufacturing cement, calcium carbonate is broken down by heat.

a i Write a word equation to show the reaction that happens inside a lime kiln.

ii What do we call this type of reaction?

b Draw a diagram to show how you could test for the gas given off in the reaction described in part a.

c Write a word equation to show the reaction between calcium oxide and water.

2 Write balanced symbol equations for the reactions in Question 1 parts a and c. [H]

3 a How is limestone turned into cement?

b Given cement powder, how would you make:

i mortar

ii concrete?

4 Potassium carbonate reacts with dilute hydrochloric acid. The gas given off gives a positive test for carbon dioxide.

a Write a word equation and a balanced symbol equation to show the reaction between potassium carbonate, K_2CO_3, and dilute hydrochloric acid. [H]

b Describe what you see in a positive test for carbon dioxide.

c Explain your observations made in part **b**. Include a word equation in your answer.

d Write a balanced symbol equation for the reaction in part **c**. [H]

5 a Here is a set of instructions for making concrete:

'To make good, strong concrete, thoroughly mix together

• 4 buckets of gravel

• 3 buckets of sand

• 1 bucket of cement

When you have done this, add half a bucket of water.'

Design and fill in a table to show the percentage of each substance in the concrete mixture. Give your values to the nearest whole number.

b Describe an investigation you could use to find out which particular mixture of gravel, sand and cement makes the strongest concrete. What would you vary, what would you keep the same and how would you test the 'strength' of the concrete?

6 In an investigation into the behaviour of carbonates, a student draws the following conclusions when he heats samples of carbonates with a Bunsen burner:

Calcium carbonate	✓
Sodium carbonate	✗
Potassium carbonate	✗
Magnesium carbonate	✓
Zinc carbonate	✓
Copper carbonate	✓

(✓ = decomposes, ✗ = does not decompose)

a What was the independent variable in the investigation?

b To which group in the periodic table do sodium and potassium belong?

c To which group in the periodic table do magnesium and calcium belong?

d What do these conclusions suggest about the behaviour of the carbonates of elements in Group 1 and Group 2?

e Can you be certain about your answer to question d? Give reasons.

f Write a word equation for the thermal decomposition of copper carbonate.

g Write a balanced symbol equation for the thermal decomposition of magnesium carbonate. [H]

AQA Examination-style questions 🄺

1 Use words from the list to complete the sentences.

calcium carbonate   calcium hydroxide
calcium oxide   carbon dioxide

Limestone is mainly made of the compound ....
When limestone is heated strongly it decomposes
producing the gas .... and solid .... When the
solid reacts with water it produces ....   (4)

2 Match the compounds in the list with the descriptions.

calcium carbonate   copper carbonate
sodium carbonate   zinc carbonate

a When heated with a Bunsen burner it does not
decompose.   (1)

b It decomposes when heated to give zinc oxide.   (1)

c It is a blue solid that produces a black solid when
heated.   (1)

d It can be heated with clay to make cement.   (1)

3 Limestone blocks are damaged by acid rain.

Use words from the list to complete the sentences.

dissolves   escapes   produces   reacts

Calcium carbonate in the limestone .... with
acids in the rain. With sulfuric acid it ....
calcium sulfate, carbon dioxide and water. The carbon
dioxide .... into the air. The calcium sulfate
.... in the rainwater.   (4)

4 A student wanted to make calcium oxide from limestone.
The student heated a piece of limestone strongly in a
Bunsen burner flame.

a Complete the word equation for the reaction that
happened:

calcium carbonate → calcium oxide + ...   (1)

The student wanted to be sure he had made calcium
oxide. He crushed the heated limestone and added
water. The mixture got hot. The student cooled the
mixture and filtered it. This gave a colourless solution
and a white solid that was left in the filter paper.

b The student added universal indicator to the
colourless solution and it turned purple.

i Name the compound in the solution that causes
the indicator to turn purple.   (1)

ii Explain how the student's observations show
that he had made some calcium oxide by heating
limestone.   (2)

c The student added dilute hydrochloric acid to the
white solid from the filter paper.

The mixture fizzed and produced a gas that turned
limewater cloudy.

i What does this tell you about the white solid?   (1)

ii Was the student successful in changing all of the
limestone into calcium oxide? Explain your answer.
        (1)

d Write balanced equations for the three chemical
reactions that the student did.   **[H]** (3)

5 Residents living near a cement works are concerned
because more children are suffering asthma attacks.
Residents have also noticed that parked cars are
becoming dirty because of smoke particles from the
chimney.

The table shows the possible medical risk from smoke
particles.

Particle size in mm	Medical effect
Larger than 0.4	No medical risks known
0.3 and smaller	Causes asthma attacks
0.2 and smaller	May cause cancer

It is also recommended that to avoid damage to health,
the concentration of any particles should be no higher
than 2 parts per million (ppm).

Scientists were brought in to monitor the emissions
from the cement works' chimney. They positioned four
sensors around the cement works to monitor airborne
smoke particles.

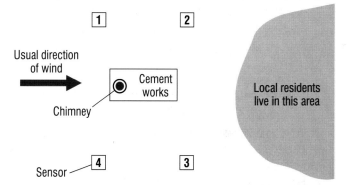

These four sensors only detect particle sizes larger than
0.5 mm and measure the concentration of particles in
ppm. The scientists reported that the particle sensors
showed that the average concentration of particles was
1.8 ppm. The scientists concluded that there was no risk
to health.

a Suggest **two** reasons why the local residents objected
to the positions of the four sensors.   (2)

b What evidence did the scientists use to conclude that
there was no risk to health?   (1)

c The local residents were still concerned that there was
a risk to health. Suggest **three** reasons why.   (3)

AQA, 2009

C1 3.1

Extracting metals

Learning objectives

● Where do metals come from?

● How can we extract metals from their ores?

Figure 1 The Angel of the North stands 20 metres tall. It is made of steel which contains a small amount of copper.

??? Did you know ...?

Gold in Wales is found in seams, just like coal – although not as thick, unfortunately! Gold jewellery was worn by early Welsh princes as a badge of rank. Welsh gold has been used in modern times to make the wedding rings of royal brides.

Figure 3 Panning for gold. Mud and stones are washed away while the dense gold remains in the pan.

Metals have been important to people for thousands of years. You can follow the course of history by the materials people used. Starting from the Stone Age, we go to the Bronze Age (copper/tin) and then on to the Iron Age.

Where do metals come from?

Metals are found in the Earth's crust. We find most metals combined chemically with other chemical elements, often with oxygen. This means that the metal must be chemically separated from its compounds before you can use it.

In some places there is enough of a metal or metal compound in a rock to make it worth extracting the metal. Then we call the rock a metal **ore**. Ores are mined from the ground. Some need to be concentrated before the metal is extracted and purified. For example, copper ores are ground up into a powder. Then they are mixed with water and a chemical that makes the copper compound repel water. Air is then bubbled through the mixture and the copper compound floats on top as a froth. The rocky bits sink and the concentrated copper compound is scraped off the top. It is then ready to have its copper extracted.

Whether it is worth extracting a particular metal depends on:

● how easy it is to extract it from its ore

● how much metal the ore contains.

These two factors can change over time. For example, a new, cheaper method might be discovered for extracting a metal. We might also discover a new way to extract a metal efficiently from rock which contains only small amounts of a metal ore. An ore that was once thought of as 'low grade' could then become an economic source of a metal.

Potassium	**Most reactive**
Sodium	
Calcium	
Magnesium	
Aluminium	
(Carbon)	
Zinc	
Iron	
Tin	
Lead	
Copper	
Silver	
Gold	
Platinum	**Least reactive**

Figure 2 This reactivity series shows how reactive each element is compared to the other elements

A few metals, such as gold and silver, are so unreactive that they are found in the Earth as the metals (elements) themselves. We say that they exist in their native state.

Sometimes a nugget of gold is so large it can simply be picked up. At other times tiny flakes have to be physically separated from sand and rocks by panning.

a If there is enough metal in a rock to make it economic to extract it, what do we call the rock?

b Why is gold found as the metal rather than combined with other elements in compounds?

How do we extract metals? *k*

The way that we extract a metal depends on its place in the **reactivity series**. The reactivity series lists the metals in order of their reactivity (see Figure 2). The most reactive are placed at the top and the least reactive at the bottom.

A more reactive metal will displace a less reactive metal from its compounds. Carbon (a non-metal) will also displace less reactive metals from their oxides. We use carbon to extract some metals from their **ores** in industry.

c A metal cannot be extracted from its ore using carbon. Where is this metal in the reactivity series?

We can find many metals, such as copper, lead, iron and zinc, combined with oxygen. The compounds are called metal oxides. Because carbon is more reactive than each of these metals, we can use carbon to extract the metals from their oxides.

We must heat the metal oxide with carbon. The carbon removes the oxygen from the metal oxide to form carbon dioxide. The metal is also formed, as the element:

metal oxide + carbon → metal + carbon dioxide

For example:

lead oxide + carbon → lead + carbon dioxide

$$2PbO + C \rightarrow 2Pb + CO_2$$

We call the removal of oxygen from a compound chemical **reduction**.

d What do chemists mean when they say that a metal oxide is reduced?

Metals that are more reactive than carbon are not extracted from their ores by reduction. Instead they are extracted using **electrolysis**.

Practical

Reduction by carbon

Heat some copper oxide with carbon powder in a test tube, gently at first then more strongly.

Empty the contents into an evaporating dish.

You can repeat the experiment with lead oxide and carbon if you have a fume cupboard to work in.

● Explain your observations. Include a word equation or a balanced symbol equation.

Summary questions

1 Copy and complete using the words below:

crust lead extracted native elements reduced

Metals come from the Earth's .... Some metals are very unreactive and are found as ...., in their .... state. Metals, such as zinc, iron and ...., are found combined with oxygen in compounds. These metals can be .... using chemical reactions. The metal oxides are .... as oxygen is removed from the compound.

2 Define the word 'ore'.

3 Platinum is never found combined with oxygen. What does this tell you about its reactivity? Give a use of platinum that depends on this property.

4 Zinc oxide (ZnO) can be reduced to zinc by heating it in a furnace with carbon. Carbon monoxide (CO) is given off in the reaction.
   a Write a word equation for the reduction of zinc oxide.
   b Now write a balanced symbol equation for the reaction in part a. **[H]**

Key points

● A metal ore contains enough of the metal to make it economic to extract the metal. Ores are mined and might need to be concentrated before the metal is extracted and purified.

● We can find gold and other unreactive metals in their native state.

● The reactivity series helps us decide the best way to extract a metal from its ore. The oxides of metals below carbon in the series can be reduced by carbon to give the metal element.

● Metals more reactive than carbon *cannot* be extracted from their ores using carbon.

C1 3.2

Iron and steels

Learning objectives

- How is iron ore reduced?
- Why is iron from a blast furnace not very useful?
- How is iron changed to make it more useful?
- What are the main types of steel?

Iron ore contains iron combined with oxygen in iron oxide. Iron is less reactive than carbon. So we can extract iron by using carbon to remove oxygen from the iron(III) oxide in the ore. We extract iron in a **blast furnace**.

Some of the iron(III) oxide reacts with carbon. The carbon reduces iron(III) oxide, forming molten iron and carbon dioxide gas. This is one of the reduction reactions which takes place in a blast furnace:

$$\text{iron(III) oxide} + \text{carbon} \rightarrow \text{iron} + \text{carbon dioxide}$$

Iron straight from the blast furnace has limited uses. It contains about 96% iron and contains impurities, mainly carbon. This makes it very brittle, although it is very hard and can't be easily compressed. When molten it can be run into moulds and cast into different shapes. This **cast iron** is used to make wood-burning stoves, man-hole covers on roads, and engines.

We can treat the iron from the blast furnace to remove some of the carbon.

Removing all the carbon and other impurities from cast iron gives us pure iron. This is very soft and easily-shaped. However, it is too soft for most uses. If we want to make iron really useful we have to make sure that it contains tiny amounts of other elements. These include carbon and metals, such as nickel and chromium.

We call a metal that is mixed with other elements an **alloy**.

Steel is an alloy of iron. By adding elements in carefully controlled amounts, we can change the properties of the steel.

> **a** Why is iron from a blast furnace very brittle?
> **b** Why is pure iron not very useful?
> **c** How do we control the properties of steel?

Steels

Steel is not a single substance. Like all alloys, it is a mixture. There are lots of different types of steel. All of them are alloys of iron with carbon and/or other elements.

Carbon steels

The simplest steels are the **carbon steels**. We make these by removing most of the carbon from cast iron, just leaving small amounts of carbon (from 0.03% to 1.5%). These are the cheapest steels to make. We use them in many products, such as the bodies of cars, knives, machinery, ships, containers and structural steel for buildings.

Often these carbon steels have small amounts of other elements in them as well. High carbon steel, with a relatively high carbon content, is very strong but brittle. On the other hand, low carbon steel is soft and easily shaped. It is not as strong, but is much less likely to shatter on impact with a hard object.

Mild steel is one type of low carbon steel. It contains less than 0.1% carbon. It is very easily pressed into shape. This makes it particularly useful in mass production, such as making car bodies.

Figure 1 The iron which has just come out of a blast furnace contains about 96% iron. The main impurity is carbon.

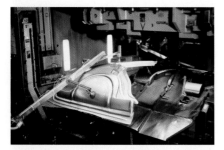

Figure 2 Low carbon steel called mild steel is easily pressed into shapes

Alloy steels

Low-alloy steels are more expensive than carbon steels because they contain between 1% and 5% of other metals. Each of these metals produces a steel that is well-suited for a particular use.

Figure 3 The properties of steel alloys make them ideal for use in suspension bridges

Even more expensive are the **high-alloy steels**. These contain a much higher percentage of other metals. The chromium–nickel steels are known as **stainless steels**. We use them to make cooking utensils and cutlery. They are also used to make chemical reaction vessels. That's because they combine hardness and strength with great resistance to corrosion. Unlike most other steels, they do not rust!

Figure 4 The properties of stainless steels make them ideal for making utensils and cutlery

 **Examiner's tip**

Know how the hardness of steels is related to their carbon content.

Summary questions

1 Copy and complete the following sentences using the terms below:

carbon   pure   steel   cast   reduced

Iron(III) oxide is .... (has its oxygen removed) in a blast furnace.

Iron from the blast furnace, poured into moulds and left to solidify is called .... iron.

If all the carbon and other impurities are removed from cast iron we get .... iron.

Iron that has been alloyed with carbon and other elements is called ....

Iron that contains just a small percentage of carbon is called .... steel.

2 How does cast iron differ from pure iron?

3 a Make a table to summarise the properties and some uses of low carbon steel, high carbon steel and chromium–nickel steel.

b Why are surgical instruments made from steel containing chromium and nickel?

Key points

- We extract iron from iron ore by reducing it using carbon in a blast furnace.

- Pure iron is too soft for it to be very useful.

- Carefully controlled quantities of carbon and other elements are added to iron to make alloys of steel with different properties.

- Important examples of steels are:
  - low carbon steels which are easily shaped,
  - high carbon steels which are very hard,
  - stainless steels which are resistant to corrosion.

C1 3.3

Aluminium and titanium

Learning objectives

- Why are aluminium and titanium so useful?

- What method is used to extract metals that are more reactive than carbon?

- Why does it cost so much to extract aluminium and titanium?

Although they are very strong, many metals are also very dense. This means that we cannot use them if we want to make something that has to be both strong and light. Examples are alloys for making an aeroplane or the frame of a racing bicycle.

Where we need metals which are both strong and have a low density, **aluminium** and **titanium** are often chosen. These are also metals which do not corrode.

Properties and uses of aluminium

Aluminium is a silvery, shiny metal. It is surprisingly light for a metal as it has a relatively low density. It is an excellent conductor of energy and electricity. We can also shape it and draw it into wires very easily.

Although aluminium is a relatively reactive metal, it does not corrode easily. This is because the aluminium atoms at its surface react with oxygen in air. They form a thin layer of aluminium oxide. This layer stops any further corrosion taking place.

Aluminium is not a particularly strong metal, but we can use it to form alloys. These alloys are harder, more rigid and stronger than pure aluminium.

Because of these properties, we use aluminium to make a whole range of goods. These include:

- drinks cans
- cooking foil
- saucepans
- high-voltage electricity cables
- aeroplanes and space vehicles
- bicycles.

Figure 1 We use aluminium alloys to make bicycles because of their combination of low density and strength

a Why does aluminium resist corrosion?
b How do we make aluminium stronger?

Extracting aluminium

Because aluminium is a reactive metal we cannot use carbon to displace it from its oxide. Instead we extract aluminium using electrolysis. An electric current is passed through molten aluminium oxide at high temperatures to break it down.

First we must mine the aluminium ore. This contains aluminium oxide mixed with impurities. Then the aluminium oxide is separated from the impurities. The oxide must then be melted before electrolysis can take place.

The problem with using electrolysis to extract metals is that it is a very expensive process. That's because we need to use high temperatures to melt the metal compound. Then we also need a great deal of electricity to extract the metal from its molten compound. There are also environmental issues to consider when using so much energy.

Figure 2 We use aluminium alloys to make aircraft. The alloys are strong yet have a low density so the plane can carry more passengers and cargo.

Properties and uses of titanium

Titanium is a silvery-white metal. It is very strong and very resistant to corrosion. Like aluminium it has an oxide layer on its surface that protects it. Although it is denser than aluminium, it is less dense than most other metals.

Titanium has a very high melting point – about 1660 °C – so we can use it at very high temperatures.

We use titanium for:

- the bodies of high-performance aircraft and racing bikes (because of its combination of strength and relatively low density)
- parts of jet engines (because it keeps its strength even at high temperatures)
- parts of nuclear reactors (where it can stand up to high temperatures and its tough oxide layer means that it resists corrosion)
- replacement hip joints (because of its low density, strength and resistance to corrosion).

> **c** What properties make titanium ideal to use in jet engines and nuclear reactors?

Extracting titanium

Titanium is not particularly reactive, so we could produce it by displacing it from its oxide with carbon. But unfortunately carbon reacts with titanium metal making it very brittle. So we have to use a more reactive metal to displace titanium. We use sodium or magnesium. However, both sodium and magnesium have to be extracted by electrolysis themselves in the first place.

Before displacement of titanium can take place, the titanium ore must be processed. This involves separating the titanium oxide and converting it to a chloride. Then the chloride is distilled to purify it. Only then is it ready for the titanium to be displaced by the sodium or magnesium. Each one of these steps takes time and costs money.

> **d** Why do we need electricity to make:
> **i** aluminium and **ii** titanium?

Figure 3 We can use titanium inside the body as well as outside. This is an artificial hip joint, used to replace a natural joint damaged by disease or wear and tear.

∞ links

For more information on the environmental impact of extracting metals, see C1 3.6 Metallic issues.

Summary questions

1 Copy and complete using the words below:

   corrode   energy   expensive   high   low   oxide   reactive   strong

   Aluminium and titanium alloys are useful as they are .... and have a .... density. Although aluminium is reactive, it does not .... because its surface is coated with a thin, tough layer of aluminium .... Titanium does not corrode because it is not very .... and also has its oxide layer to protect it. We use large amounts of .... in the extraction of both metals from their ores which makes them .... The large number of steps involved in the extraction of the metals also contributes to their .... cost.

2 Why is titanium used to make artificial hip joints?

3 **a** Explain the different reasons why carbon cannot be used to extract:
   i aluminium, or **ii** titanium.
   b Name two processes in the extraction of aluminium that require large amounts of energy.

Key points

- Aluminium and titanium are useful because they resist corrosion.

- Aluminium requires the electrolysis of molten aluminium oxide to extract it as it is too reactive to reduce using carbon.

- Aluminium and titanium are expensive because extracting them from their ores involves many stages and requires large amounts of energy.

C1 3.6 Metallic issues

Learning objectives

- What issues arise in exploiting metal ores?
- How can plants help to exploit low-grade metal ores?
- Why should we recycle metals?
- What are the good and bad points in using metals to build structures?

Exploiting metal ores

It is difficult to imagine our lives without metals. They play a vital role in our technological society. Just think of all those electrical devices we depend on! However, whenever we mine metal ores from the Earth's crust there are consequences for our environment.

You have seen that open cast mining is often used to get copper ore from the ground. The ores of iron and aluminium are also mainly mined like this. Huge pits that scar the landscape are made, creating noise and dust and destroying the habitats of plants and animals. The mines also leave large heaps of waste rock.

The water in an area can also be affected by mining. As rain drains through exposed ores and slag heaps of waste, the groundwater can become acidic.

Then the ores must be processed to extract the metals. For example, sulfide ores are heated strongly in smelting. Any sulfur dioxide gas that escapes into the air will cause acid rain.

Phytomining

As plants grow, they absorb dissolved ions in the soil through their roots. Some plants are very effective at absorbing metal ions. Once harvested, we can extract the metals from ash left after burning the plants. This can be used in the phytomining of low-grade metal ores, such as copper ores.

Copper metal is extracted from the plant by dissolving the ash in sulfuric acid first of all. Then the solution made can be electrolysed to get the copper. The copper collects at the negative electrode. Alternatively, scrap iron can be added to the solution to displace copper:

$$\text{iron} + \text{copper sulfate} \rightarrow \text{iron sulfate} + \text{copper}$$

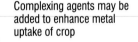

Complexing agents may be added to enhance metal uptake of crop

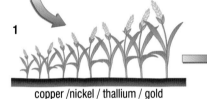

1 copper /nickel / thallium / gold
Crop grows on soil containing metal concentration too low for conventional exploitation

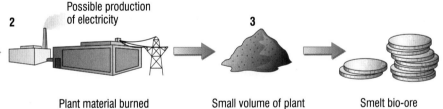

Possible production of electricity

2 Plant material burned

3 Small volume of plant ash (bio-ore) containing high concentration of target metal

Smelt bio-ore to yield metal

Figure 1 Metal ions are absorbed by plants which can then be processed to extract the metals

⬯ links

For more information on open cast copper mining and phytomining, look back at C1 3.4 Extracting copper.

Recycling metals

In the UK each person uses around 8 kg of aluminium every year. This is why it is important to **recycle** aluminium. It saves energy, and therefore money, since recycling aluminium does not involve electrolysis. Comparing recycled aluminium with aluminium extracted from its ore, there is a 95% energy saving.

We also recycle iron and steel. 'Tin cans' are usually steel cans with a very thin coating of tin to prevent rusting. These cans are easy to separate from rubbish as they are magnetic. Using recycled steel saves about 50% of the energy used to extract iron and turn it into steel. Much of this energy is supplied by burning fossil fuels so recycling helps save our dwindling supplies of the fuels.

Copper is also recycled but this is tricky as it is often alloyed with other metals. So it would need to be purified for use in electrical wiring.

Recycling metals reduces the need to mine the metal ore and conserves the Earth's reserves of metal ores. It also prevents any pollution problems that arise from extracting the metal from its ore.

Metallic structures

Steel is the most commonly used metal. It is often used in the construction industry where strength is needed. For example:

- skyscrapers have steel girders supporting them
- suspension bridges use thick steel cables
- concrete bridges over motorways are made from concrete, reinforced with steel rods.

However, steel does have some drawbacks. Unfortunately the iron in it tends to rust. Stainless steel could be used but only for small specialist jobs. That's because it is much more expensive than ordinary steel. Even so, protecting the steel from rusting also costs money. Coatings, such as paint or grease, also have to be reapplied regularly. Rusting will affect the strength of steel and can be dangerous.

Figure 2 Recycling cans saves energy and reduces pollution

Figure 3 The Golden Gate Bridge in San Francisco uses thick steel cables to support it

Some benefits of using metals in construction	Some drawbacks of using metals in construction
<ul><li>Copper is a good electrical conductor for wiring; it is not reactive so can be made into water pipes</li><li>Lead can be bent easily so is used to seal joints on roofs</li><li>Steel is strong for girders and scaffolding</li><li>Aluminium alloys are corrosion-resistant.</li></ul>	<ul><li>Iron and steel can rust, severely weakening structures, e.g. if the iron rods used inside reinforced concrete rust, structures can collapse</li><li>The exploitation of metal ores to extract metals causes pollution and uses up the Earth's limited resources</li><li>Metals are more expensive than other materials such as concrete.</li></ul>

Activity

Saving energy

Make a list of the processes required in one of the following:

- extracting iron from its ore and then making steel
- extracting aluminium from its ore
- recycling steel or aluminium.

Highlight those processes that use a lot of energy. Then write a paragraph justifying the claims that recycling metal saves energy.

Summary questions

1 What can a mining company do to help the environment when an open-cast mine is no longer economic?

2 Each person in the UK uses about 8 kg of aluminium each year.
   a Recycling 1 kg of aluminium saves about enough energy to run a small electric fire for 14 hours. If you recycle 50% of the aluminium you use in one year, how long could you run a small electric fire on the energy you have saved?
   b Explain the benefits of recycling aluminium.

Key points

- There are social, economic and environmental issues associated with exploiting metal ores.
- Plants can remove metals from low-grade ores. The metals can be recovered by processing the ash from burning the plants.
- Recycling metals saves energy and our limited metal ores (and fossil fuels). The pollution from extracting metals is also reduced.
- There are drawbacks as well as benefits from the use of metals in structures.

Summary questions 🄚

1 Write simple definitions for the following terms:
   a metal ore
   b native state
   c chemical reduction.

2 We can change the properties of metals by alloying them with other elements.

   Write down **three** ways that a metal alloy may be different from the pure metal.

3 a What name is given to the method of extracting copper from an ore:
   i using bacteria
   ii using plants
   iii using heat
   iv using electricity?

   b Which methods in part **a** are being developed to extract copper from low-grade copper ores?

4 Describe how brassicas can be used to decontaminate 'brown-field' sites and recover the polluting metals. [H]

5 Carry out some research to find the advantages and disadvantages of using bioleaching to extract copper metal.

6 By the middle of the decade scrap car dealers are required to recover 95% of all materials used to make a car. The following table shows the metals we find in an average car:

Material	Average mass (kg)	% mass
Ferrous metal (steels)	780	68.3
Light non-ferrous metal (mainly aluminium)	72	6.3
Heavy non-ferrous metal (for example lead)	17	1.5

Other materials used include plastics, rubber and glass.

a What is the average mass of metal in a car?

b What percentage of a car's mass is made up of **non-metallic** materials?

c i What is the main metal found in most cars?
   ii Which of this metal's properties allows it to be separated easily from other materials in the scrap from a car?

7 The following was overheard in a jeweller's shop:

"I would like to buy a 24-carat gold ring for my husband."

"Well madam, we would advise that you buy one which is a lower carat gold. It looks much the same but the more gold there is, the softer it is."

Is this actually the case? Let's have a look scientifically at the data.

Pure gold is said to be 24 carats. A carat is a twenty-fourth, so $24 \times \frac{1}{24} = 1$ or pure gold. So a 9-carat gold ring will have $\frac{9}{24}$ gold and $\frac{15}{24}$ of another metal, probably copper or sometimes silver. Most 'gold' sold in shops is therefore an alloy.

How hard the 'gold' is will depend on the amount of gold and on the type of metal used to make the alloy.

Here are some data on the alloys and the maximum hardness of 'gold'.

Gold alloy (carat)	Maximum hardness (BHN)
9	170
14	180
18	230
22	90
24	70

a Which metals are used to alloy gold in jewellery?

b The shop assistant said that 'the more gold there is, the less hard it is.' Was this based on science or was it hearsay? Explain your answer.

c In this investigation which is the independent variable?

d Which type of variable is 'the maximum hardness of the alloy' – continuous or categoric?

e Plot a graph of the results.

f What is the pattern in the results?

AQA Examination-style questions (k)

1 Bicycle frames are often made from metal tubes. The metal tubes are produced using the steps in this list:

mining → concentrating → extracting → purifying → alloying → shaping

Match each of the following statements with the correct word from the list.

a The metal is produced using chemical reduction. (1)

b The metal is mixed with other metals to make it harder and stronger. (1)

c The metal ore is dug from the ground. (1)

d Waste rock is removed from the metal ore. (1)

e Other elements are removed from the metal. (1)

2 Choose the correct words from those shown to complete each sentence.

a Gold is found in the Earth as .... (1)

gold chloride   gold metal   gold oxide

b Iron is extracted by reacting iron oxide with .... (1)

carbon   copper   nitrogen

c Aluminium is extracted from aluminium oxide using .... (1)

combustion   distillation   electrolysis

3 Copper metal is used for electric wires. An alloy of copper, called brass, is used for pins and terminals of electric plugs.

a Copper metal is relatively soft and flexible. Give another reason why copper is used for electric wires. (1)

b Brass is an *alloy*. What is an *alloy*? (1)

c Open-cast mining of copper ore makes a very large hole.

  i Suggest **one** environmental problem that is caused by open-cast mining of copper ore. (1)

  ii Some copper ores contain copper sulfide, CuS. Copper sulfide in heated in air to produce copper and sulfur dioxide.

  $CuS + O_2 \rightarrow Cu + SO_2$

  Suggest **one** environmental problem caused by heating copper sulfide in air. (1)

d The amount of copper-rich ores is estimated to last only a few more years. New houses need several kilometres of copper wire.

  i Explain why the need to use so much copper will cause a problem in the future. (1)

  ii Suggest **two** ways in which society could overcome this problem. (2)

  AQA, 2008

4 *In this question you will be assessed on using good English, organising information clearly and using specialist terms where appropriate.*

Most of the iron we use is converted into steels.

Describe and explain how the differences in the properties of the three main types of steel allow them to be used in different ways. (6)

5 Titanium is used in aircraft, ships and hip replacement joints. Titanium is as strong as steel but 45% lighter, and is more resistant to acids and alkalis.

Most titanium is produced from its ore, rutile (titanium oxide), by a batch process that takes up to 17 days.

  Titanium oxide is reacted with chlorine to produce titanium chloride →

  Titanium chloride is reacted with magnesium at 900 °C in a sealed reactor for 3 days →

  The reactor is allowed to cool, then opened and the titanium is separated from the magnesium chloride by hand.

Titanium reactors produce about 1 tonne of the metal per day.

Iron blast furnaces produce about 20 000 tonnes of the metal per hour.

a Give **one** property of titanium that makes it more useful than steel for hip replacement joints. (1)

b Suggest **three** reasons why titanium costs more than steel. (3)

  AQA, 2008

6 Phytomining uses plants to absorb metal compounds from the ground. It is often used on land that has been contaminated by normal mining. It involves these stages:

Sow seeds → grow plants → harvest plants → dry plants → burn plants → collect ash

The ash is then treated like a metal ore obtained by normal mining.

a Suggest **one** environmental advantage of phytomining compared with normal mining. (1)

The table shows information about some metals that are absorbed by plants used for phytomining.

Metal	Value of metal in £ per kg	Maximum mass of metal in plants in g per kg	Percentage (%) of metal in normal ore
Gold	25 000	0.10	0.002
Nickel	17	38	2
Copper	4.9	14	0.5
Zinc	3.2	40	5
Lead	1.5	10	3

b The plants used for gold phytomining give a maximum yield of 20 tonnes of plants per hectare. Calculate the maximum value of the gold that can be recovered from 1 hectare. (2)

c One kilogram of plants used for nickel phytomining produces 150 g of ash.

  What is the percentage of nickel in the ash? (2)

d Suggest reasons why phytomining has been used to produce gold, nickel and copper, but is only rarely used to produce zinc and lead. (4)

C1 4.1 Fuels from crude oil

Some of the 21st century's most important chemicals come from crude oil. These chemicals play a major part in our lives. We use them as fuels to run our cars, to warm our homes and to make electricity.

Fuels are important because they keep us warm and on the move. So when oil prices rise, it affects us all. Countries that produce crude oil can affect the whole world economy by the price they charge for their oil.

a Why is oil so important?

Crude oil

Crude oil is a dark, smelly liquid. It is a **mixture** of lots of different chemical compounds. A mixture contains two or more elements or compounds that are not chemically combined together.

Crude oil straight from the ground is not much use. There are too many substances in it, all with different boiling points. Before we can use crude oil, we must separate it into different substances with similar boiling points. These are known as **fractions**. Because the properties of substances do not change when they are mixed, we can separate mixtures of substances in crude oil by using **distillation**. Distillation separates liquids with different boiling points.

b What is crude oil?
c Why can we separate crude oil using distillation?

Figure 1 The price of nearly everything we buy is affected by oil because the cost of moving goods to the shops affects the price we pay for them

Demonstration

Distillation of crude oil

Mixtures of liquids can be separated using distillation. This can be done in the lab on a small scale. We heat the crude oil mixture so that it boils. The different fractions vaporise between different ranges of temperature. We can collect the vapours by cooling and condensing them.

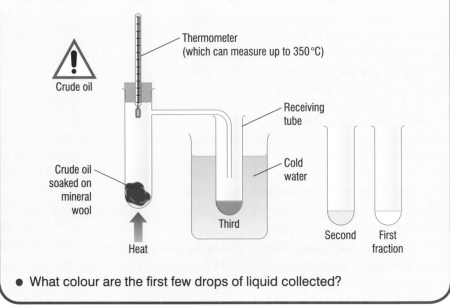

● What colour are the first few drops of liquid collected?

Hydrocarbons 🄚

Nearly all of the compounds in crude oil are compounds containing only hydrogen and carbon. We call these compounds **hydrocarbons**. Most of the hydrocarbons in crude oil are **alkanes**. You can see some examples of alkane molecules in Figure 2.

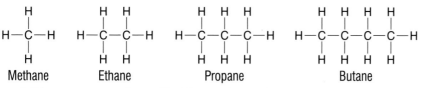

Figure 2 We can represent alkanes like this, showing all of the atoms in the molecule. They are called displayed formulae. The line drawn between two atoms in a molecule represents the covalent bond holding them together.

Look at the formulae of the first five alkane molecules:

CH_4 (methane)

C_2H_6 (ethane)

C_3H_8 (propane)

C_4H_{10} (butane)

C_5H_{12} (pentane).

Can you see a pattern in the formulae of the alkanes? We can write the general formula for alkane molecules like this:

$$C_nH_{(2n + 2)}$$

which means that 'for every n carbon atoms there are (2n + 2) hydrogen atoms'. For example, if an alkane contains 12 carbon atoms its formula will be $C_{12}H_{26}$.

We describe alkanes as **saturated hydrocarbons**. This means that they contain as many hydrogen atoms as possible in each molecule. No more hydrogen atoms can be added.

🔗 **links**

For information on covalent bonding, look back at C1 1.4 Forming bonds.

🔗 **links**

For more information on organic compounds, see C3 5.1 Structures of alcohols, carboxylic acids and esters.

Summary questions

1 Copy and complete using the words below:

   carbon   distillation   hydrocarbons   hydrogen   mixture

   Crude oil is a .... of compounds. Many of these only contain atoms of .... and .... They are called .... The compounds in crude oil can be separated using ....

2 We drill crude oil from the ground or seabed. Why is this crude oil not very useful as a product itself?

3 **a** Write the formulae of the alkanes which have 6 to 10 carbon atoms. Then find out their names.

   b Draw the displayed formula of pentane (see Figure 2).

   c How many carbon atoms are there in an alkane which has 30 hydrogen atoms?

Key points

- Crude oil is a mixture of many different compounds.

- Many of the compounds in crude oil are hydrocarbons – they contain only hydrogen and carbon.

- Alkanes are saturated hydrocarbons. They contain as many hydrogen atoms as possible in their molecules.

C1 4.2

Fractional distillation

The compounds in crude oil

Hydrocarbon molecules can be very different. Some are quite small, with relatively few carbon atoms in short chains. These short-chain molecules are the hydrocarbons that tend to be most useful. They make good fuels as they burn well. They are very **flammable**. Other hydrocarbons have lots of carbon atoms, and may have branches or side-chains.

The boiling point of a hydrocarbon depends on the size of its molecules. We can use the differences in boiling points to separate the hydrocarbons in crude oil.

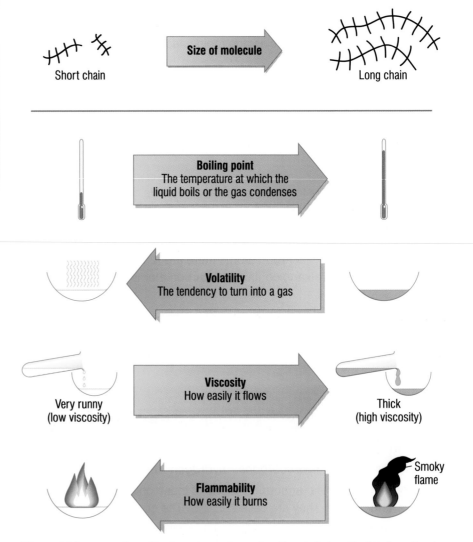

Figure 1 The properties of hydrocarbons depend on the chain-length of their molecules

a How does the length of the hydrocarbon chain affect:
   i the boiling point
   ii the viscosity (thickness) of a hydrocarbon?
b A hydrocarbon catches fire very easily. Is it likely to have molecules with long hydrocarbon chains or short ones?

Fractional distillation of crude oil 🄚

We separate out crude oil into hydrocarbons with similar boiling points, called fractions. We call this process **fractional distillation**. Each hydrocarbon fraction contains molecules with similar numbers of carbon atoms. Each of these fractions boils at a different temperature range. That is because of the different sizes of their molecules.

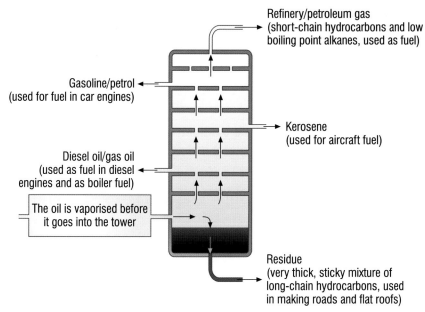

Refinery/petroleum gas
(short-chain hydrocarbons and low boiling point alkanes, used as fuel)

Gasoline/petrol
(used for fuel in car engines)

Kerosene
(used for aircraft fuel)

Diesel oil/gas oil
(used as fuel in diesel engines and as boiler fuel)

The oil is vaporised before it goes into the tower

Residue
(very thick, sticky mixture of long-chain hydrocarbons, used in making roads and flat roofs)

Figure 2 We use fractional distillation to separate the mixture of hydrocarbons in crude oil into fractions. Each fraction contains hydrocarbons with similar boiling points.

Crude oil is fed in near the bottom of a tall tower (a fractionating column) as hot vapour. The column is kept very hot at the bottom and much cooler at the top. The temperature decreases going up the column. The gases condense when they reach the temperature of their boiling points. So the different fractions are collected as liquids at different levels. Crude oil enters the fractionating column and fractions are collected in a continuous process.

Hydrocarbons with the smallest molecules have the lowest boiling points. They are collected at the cool top of the column. At the bottom of the column, the fractions have high boiling points. They cool to form very thick liquids or solids at room temperature.

Once collected, the fractions need more processing before they can be used.

⁇ Did you know … ?

A quarter of the world's reserves of crude oil are found in Saudi Arabia.

There are many different types of crude oil. For example, crude oil from Venezuela contains many long-chain hydrocarbons. It is very dark and thick and we call it 'heavy' crude. Other countries, such as Nigeria and Saudi Arabia, produce crude oil which is much paler in colour and runnier. This is 'light' crude.

Figure 3 An oil refinery at night

Summary questions

1 Copy and complete using the words below:

   easily distillation fractions high mixture viscosity

   Crude oil is a .... of many different hydrocarbons. We can separate crude oil into different .... using fractional .... A hydrocarbon molecule with many carbon atoms will have a .... boiling point and .... Hydrocarbon molecules with few carbon atoms catch fire .... and burn with a cleaner flame.

2 a Explain the steps involved in the fractional distillation of crude oil.
   b Make a table to summarise how the properties of hydrocarbons depend on the size of their molecules.

Key points

- We separate crude oil into fractions using fractional distillation.

- The properties of each fraction depend on the size of their hydrocarbon molecules.

- Lighter fractions make better fuels as they ignite more easily and burn well, with cleaner (less smoky) flames.

C1 4.3 Burning fuels (k)

Learning objectives

- What are the products of combustion when we burn fuels in a good supply of air?
- What pollutants are produced when we burn fuels?

⊂⊃ links

For information on useful fractions from crude oil, look back at C1 4.2 Fractional distillation.

Figure 1 On a cold day we can often see the water produced when fossil fuels burn

The lighter fractions from crude oil are very useful as fuels. When hydrocarbons burn in plenty of air they release energy. The reaction produces two new substances – carbon dioxide and water.

For example, when propane burns we can write:

$$propane + oxygen \rightarrow carbon\ dioxide + water$$

or

$$C_3H_8 + 5O_2 \rightarrow 3CO_2 + 4H_2O$$

The carbon and hydrogen in the fuel are **oxidised** completely when they burn like this. 'Oxidised' means adding oxygen in a chemical reaction in which oxides are formed.

Practical

Products of combustion

We can test the products given off when a hydrocarbon burns as shown in Figure 2.

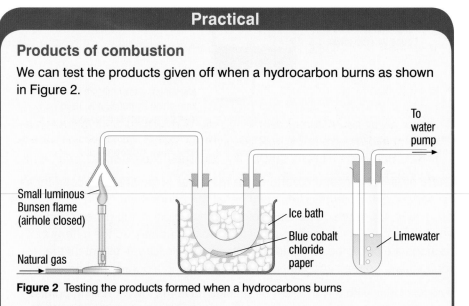

Figure 2 Testing the products formed when a hydrocarbons burns

- What happens to the limewater?
  Which gas is given off?
- What happens in the U-tube?
  Which substance is present?

---

a What are the names of the two substances produced when hydrocarbons burn in plenty of air?

b Methane is the main gas in natural gas. Write a word equation for methane burning in plenty of air.

Pollution from fuels

All fossil fuels – oil, coal and natural gas – produce carbon dioxide and water when they burn in plenty of air. But as well as hydrocarbons, these fuels also contain other substances. Impurities containing sulfur found in fuels cause us major problems.

All fossil fuels contain at least some sulfur. This reacts with oxygen when we burn the fuel. It forms a gas called **sulfur dioxide**. This gas is poisonous. It is also acidic. This is bad for the environment, as it is a cause of acid rain. Sulfur dioxide can also cause engine corrosion.

> **c** When fuels burn, what element present in the impurities in a fossil fuel may produce sulfur dioxide?
>
> **d** Which pollution problem does sulfur dioxide gas contribute to?

When we burn fuels in a car engine, even more pollution can be produced.

- When there is not enough oxygen inside an engine, we get **incomplete combustion**. Instead of all the carbon in the fuel turning into carbon dioxide, we also get **carbon monoxide** gas (CO) formed.

  Carbon monoxide is a poisonous gas. Your red blood cells pick up this gas and carry it around in your blood instead of oxygen. So even quite small amounts of carbon monoxide gas are very bad for you.

- The high temperature inside an engine also allows the nitrogen and oxygen in the air to react together. This reaction makes **nitrogen oxides**. These are poisonous and can trigger some people's asthma. They also cause acid rain.

- Diesel engines burn hydrocarbons with much bigger molecules than petrol engines. When these big molecules react with oxygen in an engine they do not always burn completely. Tiny solid particles containing carbon and unburnt hydrocarbons are produced. These **particulates** get carried into the air. Scientists think that they may damage the cells in our lungs and even cause cancer.

Figure 3 A combination of many cars in a small area and the right weather conditions can cause smog to be formed. This is a mixture of SMoke and fOG.

Key points

- When we burn hydrocarbon fuels in plenty of air the carbon and hydrogen in the fuel are completely oxidised. They produce carbon dioxide and water.

- Sulfur impurities in fuels burn to form sulfur dioxide which can cause acid rain.

- Changing the conditions in which we burn hydrocarbon fuels can change the products made.

- In insufficient oxygen, we get poisonous carbon monoxide gas formed. We can also get particulates of carbon (soot) and unburnt hydrocarbons, especially if the fuel is diesel.

- At the high temperatures in engines, nitrogen from the air reacts with oxygen to form nitrogen oxides. These cause breathing problems and can cause acid rain.

Summary questions

1 Copy and complete using the words below:

monoxide   carbon   nitrogen   oxidised   particulates   sulfur   water

When hydrocarbons burn in a good supply of air, ... dioxide and .... are made, as the carbon and hydrogen in the fuel are .... As well as these compounds other substances such as .... dioxide may be made which causes acid rain. Other pollutants that may be formed include .... oxides, carbon .... and ....

2 Explain how **a** sulfur dioxide **b** nitrogen oxides and **c** particulates are produced when fuels burn in vehicles.

3 **a** Natural gas is mainly methane (CH_4). Write a balanced symbol equation for the complete combustion of methane.   **[H]**

  b When natural gas burns in a faulty gas heater it can produce carbon monoxide (and water). Write a balanced symbol equation to show this reaction.   **[H]**

C1 5.1 Cracking hydrocarbons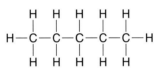

Learning objectives

- How do we make smaller, more useful molecules from larger, less useful molecules in crude oil?

- What are alkenes and how are they different from alkanes?

Figure 2 In an oil refinery, huge crackers like this are used to break down large hydrocarbon molecules into smaller ones

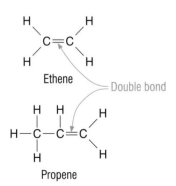

Figure 3 A molecule of ethene (C_2H_4) and a molecule of propene (C_3H_6). These are both alkenes – each molecule has a carbon–carbon double bond in it.

Some of the heavier fractions that we get by distilling crude oil are not very useful. The hydrocarbons in them are made up of large molecules. They are thick liquids or solids with high boiling points. They are difficult to vaporise and do not burn easily – so they are no good as fuels! Yet the main demand from crude oil is for fuels.

Luckily we can break down large hydrocarbon molecules in a process we call **cracking**.

The process takes place at an oil refinery in a steel vessel called a cracker.

In the cracker, a heavy fraction produced from crude oil is heated to vaporise the hydrocarbons. The vapour is then either passed over a hot catalyst or mixed with steam. It is heated to a high temperature. The hydrocarbons are cracked as thermal decomposition reactions take place. The large molecules split apart to form smaller, more useful ones.

a Why is cracking so important?
b How are large hydrocarbon molecules cracked?

Example of cracking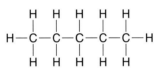

Decane is a medium-sized molecule with ten carbon atoms. When we heat it to 500 °C with a catalyst it breaks down. One of the molecules produced is pentane which is used in petrol.

Figure 1 Pentane (C_5H_{12}) can be used as a fuel. This is the displayed formula of pentane.

We also get propene and ethene which we can use to produce other chemicals.

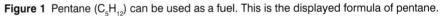

$$\underset{\text{decane}}{C_{10}H_{22}} \xrightarrow{\text{500 °C + catalyst}} \underset{\text{pentane}}{C_5H_{12}} + \underset{\text{propene}}{C_3H_6} + \underset{\text{ethene}}{C_2H_4}$$

This reaction is an example of thermal decomposition.

Notice how this cracking reaction produces different types of molecules. One of the molecules is pentane. The first part of its name tells us that it has five carbon atoms (*pent-*). The last part of its name (*-ane*) shows that it is an alkane. Like all other alkanes, pentane is a saturated hydrocarbon. Its molecules have as much hydrogen as possible in them.

The other molecules in this reaction have names that end slightly differently. They end in *-ene*. We call this type of molecule an **alkene**. The different ending tells us that these molecules are **unsaturated**. They contain a **double bond** between two of their carbon atoms. Look at Figure 3. You can see that alkenes have one double bond and have the general formula C_nH_{2n}.

Practical

Cracking

Medicinal paraffin is a mixture of hydrocarbon molecules. You can crack it by heating it and passing the vapour over hot pieces of broken pot. The broken pot acts as a catalyst.

● Why must you remove the end of the delivery tube from the water before you stop heating?

If you carry out this practical, collect at least two test tubes of gas. Test one by putting a lighted splint into it. Test the other by shaking it with a few drops of bromine water.

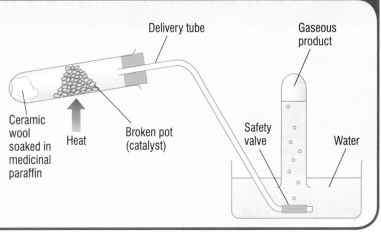

A simple experiment like the one above shows that alkenes burn. They also react with bromine water (which is orange). The products of this reaction are colourless. This means that we have a good test to see if a hydrocarbon is unsaturated:

Positive test:

unsaturated hydrocarbon + bromine water → products
                        (orange-yellow)   (colourless)

Negative test:

saturated hydrocarbon + bromine water → no reaction
                  (orange)   (orange)

Summary questions

1 Copy and complete using the words below:

alkenes catalyst cracking double heating unsaturated

Large hydrocarbon molecules are broken down by .... them and passing them over a hot .... This is called .... Some of the molecules produced when we do this contain a .... bond. They are called .... hydrocarbons. They are examples of a group of hydrocarbons called the ....

2 Cracking a hydrocarbon makes two new hydrocarbons, A and B. When bromine water is added to A, nothing happens. Bromine water added to B turns from an orange solution to colourless.
  a Which hydrocarbon is unsaturated?
  b Which hydrocarbon is used as a fuel?
  c What type of reaction is cracking an example of?
  d Cracking can be carried out by passing large hydrocarbon molecules over a hot catalyst. State another way to crack a hydrocarbon in industry.

3 An alkene molecule with one double bond contains 7 carbon atoms. How many hydrogen atoms does it have? Write down its formula.

4 Decane (with 10 carbon atoms) is cracked into octane (with 8 carbon atoms) and ethene. Write a balanced equation for this reaction. **[H]**

??? Did you know ... ?

Ethene gas makes fruits such as bananas ripen. Bananas are picked and stored as the unripe green fruit. When they are required for display in a shop ethene gas is passed over the stored bananas to start the ripening process.

AQA Examiner's tip

Remember:
alk**a**nes are s**a**turated
alk**e**nes have a double bond = (**e**quals)

Key points

● We can split large hydrocarbon molecules up into smaller molecules by:
  – mixing them with steam and heating them to a high temperature, or
  – by passing the vapours over a hot catalyst.

● Cracking produces saturated hydrocarbons which are used as fuels and unsaturated hydrocarbons (called alkenes).

● Alkenes react with orange bromine water, turning it colourless.

C1 5.3 New and useful polymers

Learning objectives

- How are we using new polymers?
- What are smart polymers?

Chemists can design new polymers to make materials with special properties to do particular jobs. Medicine is one area where we are beginning to see big benefits from these 'polymers made to order'.

New polymer materials will eventually take over from fillings for teeth which contain mercury. Working with the toxic mercury every day is a potential hazard to dental workers. Other developments include:

- new softer linings for dentures (false teeth)
- new packaging material
- implants that can slowly release drugs into a patient.

a What do we mean by a 'designer polymer'?

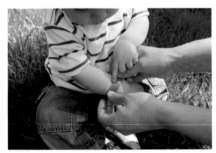

Figure 1 A sticking plaster is often needed when we cut ourselves. Getting hurt isn't much fun – and sometimes taking the plaster off can be painful too.

Light-sensitive plasters

We all know how uncomfortable pulling a plaster off your skin can be. But for some of us taking off a plaster is really painful. Both very old and very young people have quite fragile skin. But now a group of chemists has made a plaster where the 'stickiness' can be switched off before the plaster is removed. The plaster uses a light-sensitive polymer.

1 The plaster is put on just like any normal plaster.
2 To remove the plaster, the top layer is peeled away from the lower layer which stays stuck to the skin.
3 Once the lower layer is exposed to the light, the adhesive becomes less sticky, making it easy to peel off your skin.

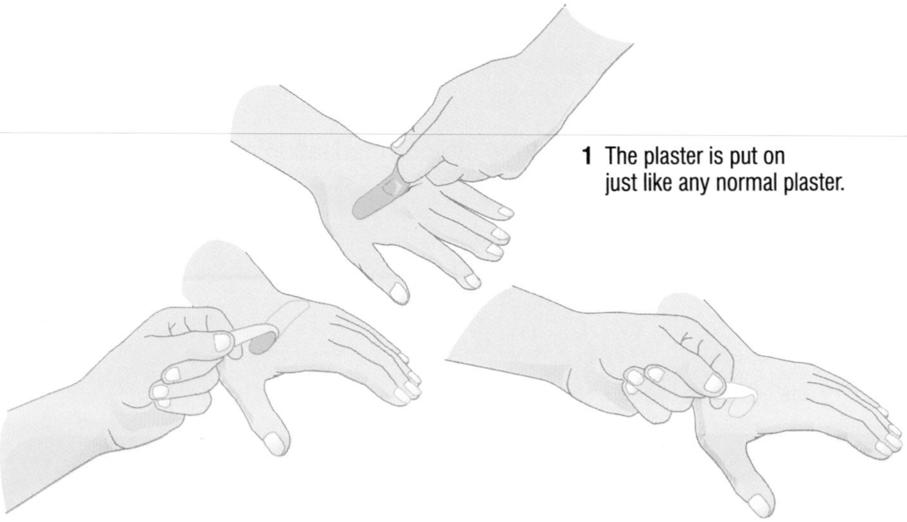

Figure 2 This plaster uses a light-sensitive polymer

How Science Works

Evaluating plastics

Plan an investigation to compare and evaluate the suitability of different plastics for a particular use.

For example, you might look at treated and untreated fabrics for waterproofing and 'breatheability' (gas permeability) or different types of packaging.

Hydrogels

Hydrogels are polymer chains with a few cross-linking units between chains. This makes a matrix that can trap water. These hydrogels are used as wound dressings. They let the body heal in moist, sterile conditions. This makes them useful for treating burns.

The latest 'soft' contact lenses are also made from hydrogels. To change the properties of hydrogels, scientists can vary the amount of water in their matrix structure.

Shape memory polymers

New polymers can also come to our rescue when we are cut badly enough to need stitches. A new 'shape memory polymer' is being developed by doctors which will make stitches that keep the sides of a cut together. When a shape memory polymer is used to stitch a wound loosely, the temperature of the body makes the thread tighten and close the wound, applying just the right amount of force.

This is an example of a 'smart polymer', i.e. one that changes in response to changes around it. In this case a change in temperature causes the polymer to change its shape. Later, after the wound is healed, the polymer is designed to dissolve and is harmlessly absorbed by the body. So there will be no need to go back to the doctor to have the stitches out.

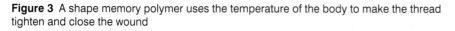

Figure 3 A shape memory polymer uses the temperature of the body to make the thread tighten and close the wound

New uses for old polymers

The bottles that we buy fizzy drinks in are a good example of using a plastic because of its properties. These bottles are made out of a plastic called PET.

The polymer it is made from is ideal for making drinks bottles. It produces a plastic that is very strong and tough, and which can be made transparent. The bottles made from this plastic are much lighter than glass bottles. This means that they cost less to transport and are easier for us to carry around.

Do you recycle your plastic bottles? The PET from recycled bottles is used to make polyester fibres for clothing, such as fleece jackets, and the filling for duvet covers. School uniforms and football shirts are now also made from recycled drinks bottles.

b Why is PET used to make drinks bottles?

Did you know ... ?

PET is an abbreviation for poly(ethene terephthalate). It takes 5 two-litre PET lemonade bottles to make one T-shirt.

links

For more information on recycling, see C1 5.4 Plastic waste.

Key points

- New polymers are being developed all the time. They are designed to have properties that make them specially suited for certain uses.

- Smart polymers may have their properties changed by light, temperature or by other changes in their surroundings.

- We are now recycling more plastics and finding new uses for them.

Summary questions

1 Copy and complete using the words below:

   cold hot PET properties shape strong transparent

   We choose a polymer for a job because it has certain .... For example, we make drinks bottles out of a plastic called .... because it is .... and ....
   Scientists can also design 'smart' polymers, for example .... memory polymers. These change their shape when they are .... or ....

2 **a** Give one advantage of using a polymer in sticking plasters that is switched off by light making the polymer less sticky.

   b Design a leaflet for a doctor to give to a patient, explaining how stitches made from smart polymers work.

C1 5.4 Plastic waste

Learning objectives

- What are the problems caused by disposing of plastics?
- What does biodegradable mean?
- How can polymers be made biodegradable?

One of the problems with plastics is what to do with them when we've finished with them. Too much ends up as rubbish in our streets. Even the beaches in the remotest parts of the world can be polluted with plastic waste. Wildlife can get trapped in the waste or eat the plastics and die.

Not only that, just think of all the plastic packaging that goes in the bin after shopping. Most of it ends up as rubbish in landfill tips. Other rubbish in the tips rots away quite quickly. Microorganisms in the soil break it down. Many waste plastics last for hundreds of years before they are broken down completely. So they take up valuable space in our landfill sites. What was a useful property during the working life of the plastic (its lack of reactivity) becomes a disadvantage in a landfill site.

a Why are waste plastics proving to be a problem for us?

Figure 1 Finding space to dump and bury our waste is becoming a big problem

Biodegradable plastics 🅚

Scientists are working to solve the problems of plastic waste. We are now making more plastics that do rot away in the soil when we dump them. These plastics are called **biodegradable**. They can be broken down by microorganisms.

Scientists have found different ways to speed up the decomposition. One way uses granules of cornstarch built into the plastic. The microorganisms in soil feed on the starch. This breaks the plastic up into small pieces more quickly.

Other types of plastic have been developed that are made from plant products. A plastic called PLA, poly(lactic acid), can be made from cornstarch. The plastic is totally biodegradable. It is used in food packaging. However, it cannot be put in a microwave which limits its use in ready-meal packaging.

We can also make plastic carrier bags using PLA. In carrier bags the PLA is mixed with a traditional plastic. This makes sure the bag is strong enough but will still biodegrade a lot more quickly.

Using plastics such as PLA also helps preserve our supplies of crude oil. Remember that crude oil is the raw material for many traditional plastics, such as poly(ethene).

Figure 2 The breakdown of a biodegradable plastic. PLA can be designed to break down in a few months.

Disadvantages of biodegradable plastics

However, the use of a food crop like corn to make plastics can raise the same issues as biofuels. Farmers who sell their crops to turn into fuel and plastics could cause higher food prices. The lack of basic food supplies could result in starvation in developing countries. Another problem is the destruction of tropical forests to create more farmland. This will destroy the habitats of wildlife and could affect global warming.

Other degradable plastics used for bags will break down in light. However, they will not decompose when buried in a landfill site. Probably the best solution is to reuse the same plastic carrier bags over and over again.

⬭ links

For information on the issues of using biofuels, look back at C1 4.5 Alternative fuels.

Practical

Investigating cornstarch

Cornstarch can be fermented to make the starting material for PLA. However, cornstarch itself also has some interesting properties. You can make your own plastic material directly from cornstarch.

● How do varying the proportions of cornstarch and water affect the product?

Recycling plastics (k)

Some plastics can be recycled. Once sorted into different types they can be melted down and made into new products. This can save energy and resources.

However, recycling plastics does tend to be more difficult than recycling paper, glass or metals. The plastic waste takes up a lot of space so is awkward to transport. Sorting out plastics into their different types adds another tricky step to the process. The energy savings are less than we get with other recycled materials. It would help recyclers if they could collect the plastics already sorted. You might have seen recycling symbols on some plastic products.

⚠1	⚠2	⚠3	⚠4	⚠5	⚠6	⚠7
PET (polyethene terephthalate)	HD PE (high density poly(ethene))	PVC	LD PE	PP	PS	Others

Figure 3 These symbols could help people sort out their plastic waste to help the recycling process

b How does recycling plastic waste help conserve our supplies of crude oil?

Figure 4 Recycling is becoming part of everyday life in the UK

Activity

Sorting plastics

a Imagine you are the head of your council's waste collection department. You have to write a leaflet for householders persuading them to recycle more of their plastic waste. They will be provided with extra bins to sort the plastics out before they are collected, once every two weeks.

b Write a letter back to the council from an unhappy person who is not willing to do any more recycling than they do already.

c Take a class vote on which action, **a** or **b**, you would support.

Summary questions

1 What do we mean by a biodegradable plastic?

2 a Why are plastics whose raw materials are plants becoming more popular?

b PLA is a biodegradable plastic. What is its monomer?

3 Non-biodegradable plastics such as poly(ethene) can be made to decompose more quickly by mixing with additives. These enable the polymer chain to be broken down by reacting with oxygen. Why might this be a waste of money if the plastic is buried and compressed under other waste in a landfill site?

Key points

● Non-biodegradable plastics cause unsightly rubbish, can harm wildlife and take up space in landfill sites.

● Biodegradable plastics are decomposed by the action of microorganisms in soil. Making plastics with starch granules in their structure help the microorganisms break down a plastic.

● We can make biodegradable plastics from plant material such as cornstarch.

C1 5.5

Ethanol

Learning objectives

- What are the two methods used to make ethanol?

- What are the advantages and disadvantages of these two methods?

Ethanol is a member of the group of organic compounds called the alcohols. Its formula is C_2H_6O but it is more often written as C_2H_5OH. This shows the $-OH$ group that all alcohols have in their molecules.

Making ethanol by fermentation

Ethanol is the alcohol found in alcoholic drinks. Ethanol for drinks is made by the **fermentation** of sugar from plants. Enzymes in yeast break down the sugar into ethanol and carbon dioxide gas:

$$\text{sugar} \xrightarrow{\text{yeast}} \text{ethanol} + \text{carbon dioxide}$$
$$\text{(glucose)}$$

$$C_6H_{12}O_6 \longrightarrow 2C_2H_5OH + 2CO_2$$

a Which gas is given off when sugar is fermented?

b Yeast is a living thing. It is a type of fungus. What type of molecules in yeast enable it to ferment sugar?

Figure 1 Some people brew their own alcoholic drinks. The fermentation stage is often carried out by leaving the fermenting mixture in a warm place. The enzymes in yeast work best in warm conditions.

??? Did you know ... ?

The yeast in a fermenting mixture cannot survive in concentrations of ethanol beyond about 15%. Alcoholic spirits, such as whisky or vodka, need to be distilled to increase the ethanol content to about 40% of their volume. Ethanol in high concentrations is toxic, which is why ethanol in the lab should never be drunk!

Practical

Fermentation

In this experiment you can ferment sugar solution with yeast and test the gas given off.

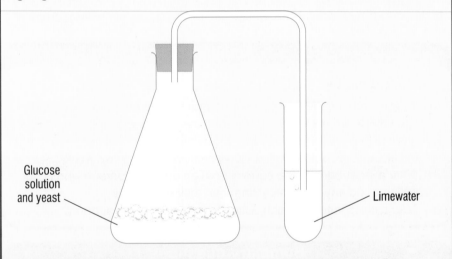

Glucose solution and yeast

Limewater

If you leave your apparatus till next lesson, your teacher can collect some fermented mixtures together and distil it to collect the ethanol formed. We use fractional distillation for the best separation as water and ethanol have similar boiling points. Ethanol boils at 78 °C. The ethanol collected will ignite and burn with a 'clean' blue flame.

∞ links

For information on using ethanol as a fuel, look back at C1 4.5 Alternative fuels.

Ethanol is also used as a solvent. Methylated spirit is mainly ethanol. Decorators can use it to clean brushes after using an oil-based paint. It is also used to make perfume. We have already seen how ethanol can be used as a fuel. It can be mixed with petrol or just used by itself to run cars.

Making ethanol from ethene (hydration)

Ethanol for industrial use as a fuel or solvent can be made from ethene gas instead of by fermentation. Remember that ethene is made when oil companies crack hydrocarbons to make fuels. Ethene is the main by-product made in cracking. Ethene gas can react with steam to make ethanol.

$$\text{ethene} + \text{steam} \xrightarrow{\text{catalyst}} \text{ethanol}$$
$$C_2H_4 + H_2O \longrightarrow C_2H_5OH$$

This reaction is called **hydration**.

CO links

For information on cracking, look back at C1 5.1 Cracking hydrocarbons.

c Where do we get the ethene from to make industrial ethanol?

The reaction requires energy to heat the gases and to generate a high pressure. The reaction is reversible so ethanol can break down back into ethene and steam. So unreacted ethene and steam need to be recycled over the catalyst.

This process is continuous. It also produces no waste products. Both of these are advantages when making products in industry. When ethanol is made industrially by fermentation, the process is carried out in large vats which have to be left. This is called a batch process, which takes a lot longer than a continuous process. Carbon dioxide, a greenhouse gas, is also given off in fermentation.

However, using ethene to make ethanol relies on crude oil which is a **non-renewable** resource. Therefore making ethanol as a biofuel, by fermenting sugars from plant material (a renewable resource), will become ever more important. The sugars are from crops such as sugar cane or sugar beet. Any cereal crop can also be used as the raw material. These need their starch to be broken down to sugars before fermentation takes place. However as we have seen before there are issues that need to be addressed when using crops for large-scale industrial processes.

Figure 2 Industrial fermentation is a slow batch process. The ethanol must be distilled off from the fermented mixture. This requires energy even though the fermentation process itself is energy efficient.

CO links

For information on the issues of using crops for large scale industrial processes, look back at C1 4.5 Alternative fuels.

Summary questions

1 Copy and complete using the words below:

   catalyst   sugar   yeast   steam

   Ethanol can be made by two processes, ethene reacting with ...., under pressure in the presence of a ...., or the fermentation of .... using enzymes in ....

2 Write a word equation to show the production of ethanol from:
   a ethene
   b glucose.

3 Why is a continuous process better than a batch process for making a product in industry?

4 How can people claim that the fermentation of plant materials does not contribute to the increase in carbon dioxide in the air?

Key points

- Ethanol can be made from ethene reacting with steam in the presence of a catalyst. This is called hydration.

- Ethanol is also made by fermenting sugar (glucose) using enzymes in yeast. Carbon dioxide is also made in this reaction.

- Using ethene to make ethanol needs non-renewable crude oil as its raw material whereas fermentation uses renewable plant material.

C1 6.1

Extracting vegetable oil

Learning objectives

- How do we extract oils from plants?

- Why are vegetable oils important foods?

- What are unsaturated oils and how do we detect them?

Plants use the Sun's energy to produce glucose from carbon dioxide and water during photosynthesis:

$$\text{carbon dioxide} + \text{water} \xrightarrow[\text{energy (from sunlight)}]{\text{chlorophyll}} \text{glucose} + \text{oxygen}$$
$$6CO_2 + 6H_2O \longrightarrow C_6H_{12}O_6 + 6O_2$$

Plants then turn glucose into other chemicals they need using more chemical reactions. In some cases these other chemicals can also be very useful to us. For example, the **vegetable oils** from plants, such as oilseed rape, make biofuels and foodstuffs.

We find these oils in the seeds of the rape plant. Farmers collect the seeds from the plants using a combine harvester. The seeds are then taken to a factory where they are crushed and pressed to extract their oil. The impurities are removed from the oil. It is then processed to make it into useful products.

We extract other vegetable oils using steam. For example, we can extract lavender oil from lavender plants by distillation. The plants are put into water and boiled. The oil and water evaporate together and are collected by condensing them. The water and other impurities are removed to give pure lavender oil.

Figure 1 Oilseed rape is a common sight in our countryside. As its name tells us, it is a good source of vegetable oil.

Practical

Extracting plant oil by distillation (microscale)

Take care not to let the contents of the small vial boil over.

- What does the liquid collected look and smell like?

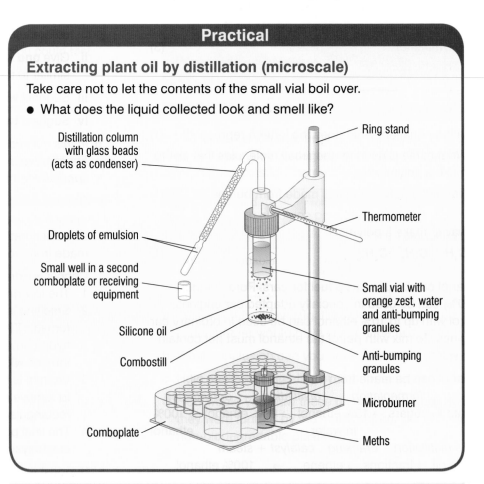

a Write down two ways we can use to extract vegetable oils from plants.

Figure 2 Norfolk lavender oil is extracted from lavender plants by distillation

Vegetable oils as foods and fuels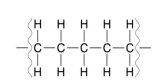

Vegetable oils are very important foods. They provide important nutrients. For example olive oil is a source of vitamin E. They also contain a great deal of energy, as the table shows. This makes them useful foods and sources of biofuels, such as biodiesel.

There are lots of different vegetable oils. Each vegetable oil contains mixtures of compounds with slightly different molecules. However, all vegetable oils have molecules which contain chains of carbon atoms with hydrogen atoms:

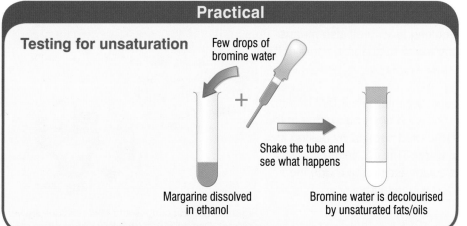

In some vegetable oils the hydrocarbon chains contain carbon–carbon double bonds (C=C). We call these **unsaturated oils**. We can detect the double bonds in unsaturated oils with bromine water. You know the test for double bonds from your work on alkenes.

This provides us with an important way of detecting unsaturated oils:

unsaturated oil + bromine water (orange) → colourless solution

> **b** What will you see if you test a polyunsaturated margarine with bromine water?

Practical

Testing for unsaturation

Few drops of bromine water

Shake the tube and see what happens

Margarine dissolved in ethanol

Bromine water is decolourised by unsaturated fats/oils

Summary questions

1 Copy and complete using the words below:

bromine   decolorised   distillation   energy   pressing   unsaturated

We can extract vegetable oils from some plants by .... or .... Vegetable oils are particularly important as foods because they contain a lot of .... Some vegetable oils contain carbon–carbon double bonds. We call these .... vegetable oils. They can be detected by reacting them with .... water, which will be ....

2 Why might a diet containing too much vegetable oil be unhealthy?

3 A sample of vegetable oils is tested with bromine water. The solution is decolorised. Which of the following statements is true?
   a The sample contains *only* unsaturated oils.
   b The sample contains *only* saturated oils.
   c The sample may contain a mixture of saturated and unsaturated oils. Explain your answer.

links

For information on biofuels, look back at C1 4.5 Alternative fuels.

| Energy in vegetable oil and other foods ||
Food	Energy in 100 g (kJ)
vegetable oil	3900
sugar	1700
animal protein (meat)	1100

Figure 3 Vegetable oils have a high energy content

links

For information on the test for double bonds, look back at C1 5.1 Cracking hydrocarbons.

Did you know ... ?

No more than 20% of the energy in your diet should come from fats.

Key points

- Vegetable oils can be extracted from plants by pressing or by distillation.

- Vegetable oils provide nutrients and have a high energy content. They are important foods and can be used to make biofuels.

- Unsaturated oils contain carbon–carbon double bonds (C=C). We can detect them as they decolorise bromine water.

Cooking with vegetable oils

Learning objectives

- What are the advantages and disadvantages of cooking with vegetable oils?

- What does it mean when we 'harden' vegetable oils? [H]

- How do we turn vegetable oils into spreads? [H]

When we cook food we heat it to a temperature where chemical reactions cause permanent changes to happen to the food. Cooking food in vegetable oil gives very different results to cooking food in water. This is because the boiling points of vegetable oils are much higher than the boiling point of water. Therefore, vegetable oils can be used at a much higher temperature than boiling water.

What's the difference?

So the chemical reactions that take place in the food are very different in oil and in water. When we cook using vegetable oil:

- the food cooks more quickly
- very often the outside of the food turns a different colour, and becomes crispier
- the inside of the food should be softer if you don't cook it for too long.

a How does the boiling point of a vegetable oil compare to the boiling point of water?

Figure 1 An electric fryer like this one enables vegetable oil to be heated safely to a high temperature

Cooking food in oil also means that the food absorbs some of the oil. As you know, vegetable oils contain a lot of energy. This can make the energy content of fried food much higher than that of the same food cooked by boiling it in water. This is one reason why regularly eating too much fried food is unhealthy.

Figure 2 Boiled potatoes and fried potatoes are very different. One thing that probably makes chips so tasty is the contrast of crispy outside and soft inside, together with the different smell and taste produced by cooking at a higher temperature. The different colour may be important too as golden chips look more appetising than a pale boiled potato.

Practical

Investigating cooking

Compare the texture and appearance of potato pieces after equal cooking times in water and oil.

You might also compare the cooking times for boiling, frying and oven-baking chips.

If possible carry out some taste tests in hygienic conditions.

AQA Examiner's tip

No chemical bonds are broken when vegetable oils melt or boil – these are physical changes.

b How is food cooked in oil different to food cooked in water?

Hardening unsaturated vegetable oils 🔉

Unsaturated vegetable oils are usually liquids at room temperature.

The boiling and melting points of these oils can be increased by adding hydrogen to the molecules. The reaction replaces some or all of the carbon–carbon double bonds with carbon–carbon single bonds.

With this higher melting point, the liquid oil becomes a solid at room temperature. We call changing a vegetable oil like this **hardening** it. We harden a vegetable oil by reacting it with hydrogen gas (H_2). To make the reaction happen, we must use a nickel catalyst, and carry it out at about 60 °C.

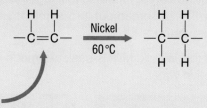

Figure 3 The hydrogen adds to the carbon–carbon double bonds in a vegetable oil when it is hardened and this can be used to make margarine

c What do we call it when we add hydrogen to a vegetable oil?

Oils that we have treated like this are sometimes called **hydrogenated oils**. They are solids at room temperature. This means that they can be made into spreads to be put on bread. We can also use them to make cakes, biscuits and pastry.

Figure 4 We can use hydrogenated vegetable oils in cooking to make a huge number of different, and delicious, foods

Summary questions

1 Copy and complete using the words below:

water energy higher tastes

The boiling points of vegetable oils are .... than the boiling point of water. This means that food cooked in oil .... different to food boiled in .... It also contains more ....

2 Copy and complete using the words below:

hydrogen hydrogenated hardening melting nickel

The .... points of oils may also be raised by adding .... to their molecules. We call this .... the oil. The reaction takes place at 60 °C in the presence of a .... catalyst. The reaction produces a .... oil. [H]

3 a Why are hydrogenated vegetable oils more useful than oils that have not been hydrogenated?

b Explain how we harden vegetable oils. [H]

Key points

● Vegetable oils are useful in cooking because of their high boiling points. However, this increases the energy content of foods compared with cooking in boiling water.

● Vegetable oils are hardened by reacting them with hydrogen to increase their melting points. This makes them solids at room temperature which are suitable for spreading. [H]

● The hardening reaction takes place at 60 °C with a nickel catalyst. The hydrogen adds onto C=C bonds in the vegetable oil molecules. [H]

C1 6.3

Everyday emulsions

Learning objectives

- What are emulsions and how do we make them?
- Why are emulsions made from vegetable oils so important?
- What is an emulsifier?
- How do emulsifiers work? [H]

Emulsions in foods

The texture of food – what it feels like in your mouth – is a very important part of foods.

Some smooth foods are made from a mixture of oil and water. Everyone knows that oil and water don't mix. Just try it by pouring a little cooking oil into a glass of water. But we can get them to mix together by making the oil into very small droplets. These spread out throughout the water and produce a mixture called an **emulsion**.

A good example of this is milk. Milk is basically made up of small droplets of animal fat dispersed in water.

Figure 1 Mayonnaise is an emulsion. Smooth food has a good texture and looks as if it will taste nice – but it is not always easy to make, or to keep it smooth.

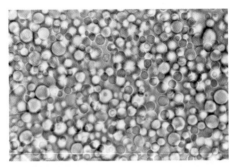

Figure 2 Milk is an emulsion made up of animal fat and water, together with some other substances

Emulsions often behave very differently to the things that we make them from. For example, mayonnaise is made from ingredients that include oil and water. Both of these are runny – but mayonnaise is not!

Another very important ingredient in mayonnaise is egg yolks. Apart from adding a nice yellow colour, egg yolks have a very important job to do in mayonnaise. They stop the oil and water from separating out into layers. Food scientists call this type of substance an **emulsifier**.

> **a** What do we mean by 'an emulsifier'?

Emulsifiers make sure that the oil and water in an emulsion cannot separate out. This means that the emulsion stays thick and smooth. Any creamy sauce needs an emulsifier. Without it we would soon find blobs of oil or fat floating around in the sauce.

> **b** How does an emulsifier help to make a good creamy sauce?

One very popular emulsion is ice cream. Everyday ice cream is usually made from vegetable oils, although luxury ice cream may also use animal fats.

Figure 3 Ice cream contains emulsifiers

Emulsifiers keep the oil and water mixed together in the ice cream while we freeze it. Without them, the water in the ice cream freezes separately, producing crystals of ice. That would make the ice cream crunchy rather than smooth. This happens if you allow ice cream to melt and then put it back in the freezer.

Other uses of emulsions

Emulsifiers are also important in the cosmetics industry. Face creams, body lotions, lipsticks and lip gloss are all emulsions.

Emulsion paint (often just called emulsion) is a water-based paint with oil droplets dispersed throughout. It is commonly used for painting indoor surfaces such as plastered walls.

Higher

How an emulsifier works

An emulsifier is a molecule with 'a tail' that is attracted to oil and 'a head' that is attracted to water. The 'tail' is a long hydrocarbon chain. This is called the **hydrophobic** part of the emulsifier molecule. The 'head' is a group of atoms that carry a charge. This is called the **hydrophilic** part of the molecule.

The 'tails' dissolve in oil making tiny droplets. The surface of each oil droplet is charged by the 'heads' sticking out into the water. As like charges repel, the oil droplets repel each other. This keeps them spread throughout the water, stopping the oil and water separating out into two layers.

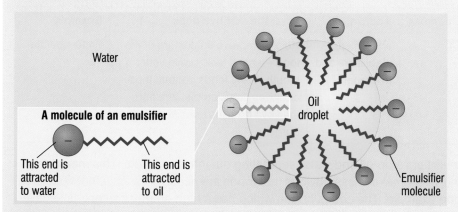

Figure 4 The structure of a typical emulsifier molecule with its water-loving (hydrophilic) head and its water-hating (hydrophobic) tail

Water

A molecule of an emulsifier

This end is attracted to water

This end is attracted to oil

Oil droplet

Emulsifier molecule

Practical

Making and testing emulsions

Detergents act as emulsifiers.

Add a little cooking oil to some water in a boiling tube. Stopper the tube and shake. Do the same in another boiling tube but also add a drop of washing-up liquid.

● Compare the mixtures when first shaken and when left standing a while.

● You can do some tests on other types of detergent to see which is the most effective emulsifier.

Key points

● Oils do not dissolve in water.

● Oils and water can be dispersed (spread out) in each other to produce emulsions which have special properties.

● Emulsions made from vegetable oils are used in many foods, such as salad dressings, ice creams, cosmetics and paints.

● Emulsifiers stop oil and water from separating out into layers.

● An emulsifier works because one part of its molecule dissolves in oil (hydrophobic part) and one part dissolves in water (hydrophilic part). [H]

Summary questions

1 Copy and complete using the words below:

emulsifier emulsion cosmetics ice mayonnaise mix separating small

Oil and water do not .... together. But if the oil droplets can be made very .... it is possible to produce a mixture of oil and water called an .... To keep the oil and water from .... we can use a chemical called an .... Important examples of food made like this include .... and .... cream. Emulsions are also important in paints and in ....

2 a Salad cream is an emulsion made from vegetable oil and water. In what ways is salad cream different from both oil and water?

   b Why do we need to add an emulsifier to an emulsion like salad cream?

3 Explain how emulsifier molecules do their job. [H]

C1 6.4

Food issues

Learning objectives

- What are the benefits and drawbacks of using emulsifiers in our food?

- What are the good and bad points about vegetable oils in our food?

Figure 1 Modern foods contain a variety of additives to improve their taste, texture or appearance, and to give them a longer shelf-life

⃝⃝ links

For information on how an emulsifier works, look back at C1 6.3 Everyday emulsions.

Emulsifying additives

For hundreds of years we have added substances like salt or vinegar to food to help keep it longer. As our knowledge of chemistry has increased we have used other substances too, to make food look or taste better.

We call a substance that is added to food to preserve it or to improve its taste, texture or appearance a **food additive**. Additives that have been approved for use in Europe are given **E numbers**. These can be used to identify them.

a What is a food additive?

Each group of additives is given a range of E numbers. These tell us what kind of additive it is. Emulsifiers are usually given E numbers in the range 400 to 500, along with stabilisers and thickeners.

E number	Additive	What the additive does	Example
E4 _ _	emulsifiers, stabilisers and thickeners	Help to improve the texture of the food – what it feels like in your mouth. Many foods contain these additives, for example, jam and the soya proteins used in veggie burgers.	E440 – pectin

Emulsifiers stop oil and water separating out into two layers. This means that emulsifiers make it less obvious that foods are rich in oil or fat. Chocolate is a good example. The cocoa butter, which has a high energy content, is usually mixed in well, often with the help of emulsifiers. However, have you ever left a bar of chocolate past its sell-by date? Then you can see a white haze on the surface of the chocolate. This is the fatty butter starting to separate out. Then most people will throw the bar away.

So emulsifiers make oil and fat more edible in foods. They can make a mixture that is creamier and thicker in texture than either oil or water. This makes it easier and more tempting for us to eat too much fatty food.

a   **b**

Figure 2 Which is more appetising – mayonnaise with emulsifier (**a**) or mayonnaise without emulsifier (**b**)?

Vegetable oils in our diet

Everyone knows the benefits of a healthy diet. But do you know the benefits of ensuring that you eat vegetable oils as part of your diet?

Scientists have found that eating vegetable oils instead of animal fats can do wonders for the health of your heart. The saturated fats you find in things like butter and cheese can make the blood vessels of your heart become clogged up.

However, the unsaturated fats in vegetable oils (like olive oil and corn oil) are very good for you. They are a source of nutrients such as vitamin E. They also help to keep your arteries clear and reduce the chance of you having heart disease. The levels of a special fat called cholesterol in your blood give doctors an idea about your risk of heart disease. People who eat vegetable oils rather than animal fats tend to have a much lower level of 'bad' cholesterol in their blood.

Figure 3 Butter contains saturated fats which raise health concerns

> **b** Name a vitamin that we get from olive oil.

The fats used to cook chips and other fast foods often contain certain fats that are not good for us. Scientists are concerned that eating these fats might have caused an increase in heart disease.

Changes in food labelling are very important. But many products, including fast foods, often contain high levels of potentially harmful fats from the oil they were cooked in. Yet these are exempt from labelling regulations and may be advertised as 'cholesterol-free' and 'cooked in vegetable oil'.

Activity

Food for thought

1 Write an article for a family lifestyle magazine about 'Feeding your family'. Include in this article reasons for including vegetable oils in a balanced diet and their effect on people's health.
2 Design a poster with the title 'Vegetable oils – good or bad'?
3 Write the script for a two-minute slot on local radio about the benefits and drawbacks of using emulsifiers in foods.

Figure 4 Chips have a high energy content and may contain potentially harmful fats from cooking oil

Key points

- Vegetable oils are high in energy and provide nutrients. They are unsaturated and believed to be better for your health than saturated animal fats and hydrogenated vegetable oils.

- Emulsifiers improve the texture of foods enabling water and oil to mix. This makes fatty foods more palatable and tempting to eat.

Summary questions

1 Draw a table to summarise the advantages and disadvantages of vegetable oils in our diet.

2 **a** Give a list of five foods that can contain emulsifiers as additives.
  b Why could it be said that emulsifiers have played a role in increasing childhood obesity rates?

Summary questions (k)

1 Write simple definitions for the following words:

   a vegetable oils

   b unsaturated oils

   c saturated oils

   d emulsion

   e emulsifier.

2 a A vegetable oil removes the colour from bromine water.

   It takes longer to decolourise the bromine water when the vegetable oil is partially hydrogenated.

   When the vegetable oil has been completely hardened it does not react with bromine water.

   Explain these observations.

   b Explain why plant oils need to be hardened and the effect this has on the melting point of the oil. **[H]**

   c Give the conditions for the reaction between a plant oil and hydrogen. **[H]**

3 Compare the cooking of a potato in boiling water and in vegetable oil.

4 a Some ice cream is left standing out on a table during a meal on a hot day. It is then put back in the freezer again. When it is taken out of the freezer a few days later, people complain that the ice cream tastes 'crunchy'. Why is this?

   b A recipe for making ice cream says: 'Stir the ice cream from time to time while it is freezing.' Why must you stir ice cream when freezing homemade ice cream?

   c Look at this list of ingredients for making ice cream:

     8 large egg yolks

     $\frac{3}{4}$ cup of sugar

     $2\frac{1}{2}$ cups of whipping cream

     $1\frac{1}{2}$ cups cold milk

     1 vanilla pod

   Which ingredient acts as an emulsifier in the mixture?

5 Draw a diagram of the structure of a typical emulsifier. **[H]**

6 State a use of vegetable oils where their high energy content is:

   a an advantage.

   b a disadvantage.

7 A teacher decided that her class should do a survey of different cooking oils to find out the degree of unsaturated oils present in them. She chose five different oils and divided them among her students. This allowed each oil to be done twice, by two different groups. They were given strict instructions as to how to do the testing.

Bromine water was added to each oil from a burette. The volume added before the mixture in the conical flask was no longer colourless was noted.

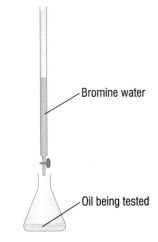

Bromine water

Oil being tested

The results are in this table.

Type of oil	Amount of bromine water added (cm³)	
	Group 1	Group 2
Ollio	24.2	23.9
Soleo	17.8	18.0
Spreo	7.9	8.1
Torneo	13.0	12.9
Margeo	17.9	17.4

   a Why was it important that the teacher gave strict instructions to all of the groups on how to carry out the tests?

   b List some control variables that should have been included in the instructions.

   c Are there any anomalous results? How did you decide?

   d What evidence is there in the results that indicate that they are reproducible?

   e How might the accuracy be checked?

   f How would you present these results on a graph? Explain your answer.

AQA Examination-style questions ⓚ

1 Vegetable oils can be extracted from parts of plants that are rich in oils.

Choose the correct word from the list to complete each sentence.

a Sunflower oil is extracted from sunflower ....

leaves   *petals*   *seeds*   (1)

b To extract olive oil the olives are crushed and ....

boiled   *evaporated*   *pressed*   (1)

c The oil may contain small pieces of solid plant material that can be removed by ....

condensing   *distilling*   *filtering*   (1)

d If the oil contains water it can be removed by leaving it to stand because oil and water ....

evaporate   *mix*   *separate*   (1)

2 Lavender oil can be extracted from lavender plants by distillation.

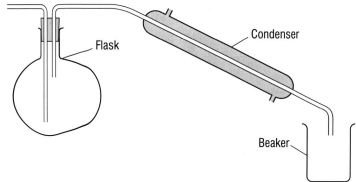

Put the following steps into the correct order, 1 to 6:

lavender plants are harvested → 1 → 2 → 3 → 4 → 5 → 6 → lavender oil is collected.

A Lavender oil and steam are condensed

B Lavender oil separates from water

C Steam is passed into the flask

D Lavender plants are put into the flask

E Lavender oil and water are collected

F Lavender oil and water evaporate   (3)

3 Potatoes cooked in boiling water take about 20 minutes to cook. Potato chips can be cooked in less than 10 minutes by deep frying in hot oil. This is one reason why fast food outlets cook chips rather than potatoes.

a Explain why chips cook faster in hot oil than in boiling water.   (2)

b Suggest another advantage for fast food outlets to cook chips.   (1)

c Suggest a disadvantage for fast food outlets cooking chips.   (1)

d Suggest an advantage for consumers who eat chips rather than boiled potatoes.   (1)

e Suggest a disadvantage for consumers who eat chips rather than boiled potatoes.   (1)

4 a A vegetable oil was shaken with water in flask 1 and with water and an emulsifier in flask 2. The diagrams show the results after leaving the mixtures to stand for 5 minutes.

Flask 1
Vegetable oil and water

Flask 2
Vegetable oil, water and an emulsifier

a i Give a reason for the result in Flask 1.   (1)
ii Explain the result in Flask 2.   (2)

b Give an example of a product that contains an emulsifier and give **two** ways in which its properties are better than those of the liquids from which it is made.   (3)

c Explain how an emulsifier works. Your answer should include a diagram of a simple model of an emulsifier molecule.   [H] (3)

AQA, 2007

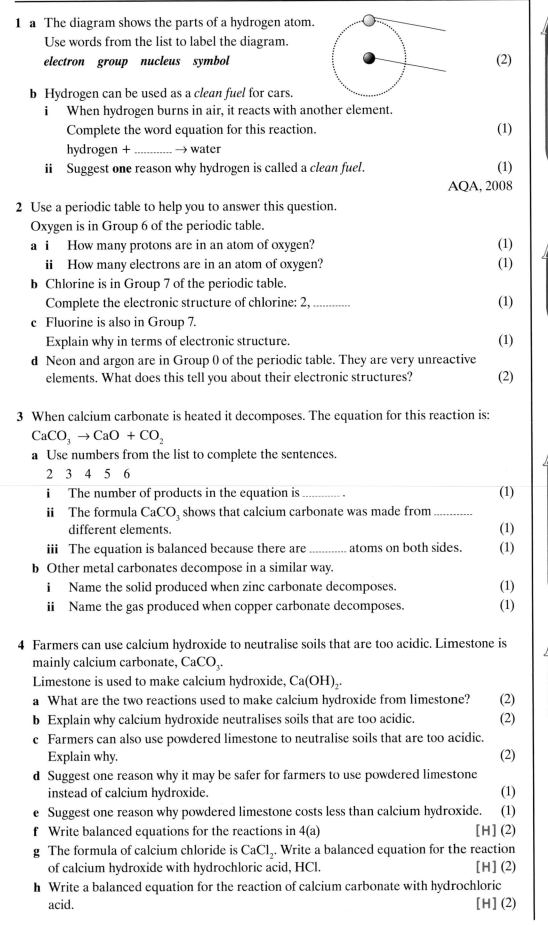

1 a The diagram shows the parts of a hydrogen atom.
Use words from the list to label the diagram.
electron   group   nucleus   symbol   (2)

   b Hydrogen can be used as a *clean fuel* for cars.
     i When hydrogen burns in air, it reacts with another element.
Complete the word equation for this reaction.   (1)
hydrogen + ... → water
    ii Suggest **one** reason why hydrogen is called a *clean fuel*.   (1)

AQA, 2008

2 Use a periodic table to help you to answer this question.
Oxygen is in Group 6 of the periodic table.
   a i How many protons are in an atom of oxygen?   (1)
    ii How many electrons are in an atom of oxygen?   (1)
   b Chlorine is in Group 7 of the periodic table.
Complete the electronic structure of chlorine: 2, ...   (1)
   c Fluorine is also in Group 7.
Explain why in terms of electronic structure.   (1)
   d Neon and argon are in Group 0 of the periodic table. They are very unreactive
elements. What does this tell you about their electronic structures?   (2)

3 When calcium carbonate is heated it decomposes. The equation for this reaction is:
$CaCO_3 \rightarrow CaO + CO_2$
   a Use numbers from the list to complete the sentences.
    2   3   4   5   6
     i The number of products in the equation is ....   (1)
    ii The formula $CaCO_3$ shows that calcium carbonate was made from ....
different elements.   (1)
   iii The equation is balanced because there are .... atoms on both sides.   (1)
   b Other metal carbonates decompose in a similar way.
     i Name the solid produced when zinc carbonate decomposes.   (1)
    ii Name the gas produced when copper carbonate decomposes.   (1)

4 Farmers can use calcium hydroxide to neutralise soils that are too acidic. Limestone is
mainly calcium carbonate, $CaCO_3$.
Limestone is used to make calcium hydroxide, $Ca(OH)_2$.
   a What are the two reactions used to make calcium hydroxide from limestone?   (2)
   b Explain why calcium hydroxide neutralises soils that are too acidic.   (2)
   c Farmers can also use powdered limestone to neutralise soils that are too acidic.
Explain why.   (2)
   d Suggest one reason why it may be safer for farmers to use powdered limestone
instead of calcium hydroxide.   (1)
   e Suggest one reason why powdered limestone costs less than calcium hydroxide.   (1)
   f Write balanced equations for the reactions in 4(a)   **[H]** (2)
   g The formula of calcium chloride is $CaCl_2$. Write a balanced equation for the reaction
of calcium hydroxide with hydrochloric acid, HCl.   **[H]** (2)
   h Write a balanced equation for the reaction of calcium carbonate with hydrochloric
acid.   **[H]** (2)

5 Titanium is as strong as steel but is much more expensive. It is used to make jet engines for aircraft and to make replacement hip joints for people.

  a Give two properties that make titanium better than steel for making jet engines and replacement hip joints. (2)

  b *In this question you will be assessed on using good English, organising information clearly and using specialist terms where appropriate.*

    Titanium is made in batches of about 10 tonnes that take up to 15 days. The main steps to make titanium are:
  * Titanium oxide is reacted with chlorine to produce titanium chloride.
  * Titanium chloride is reacted with magnesium at 900 °C in a sealed reactor for three days to give a mixture of titanium and magnesium chloride.
  * The reactor is cooled for seven days, and then the mixture is removed.
  * The magnesium chloride is removed from the mixture by distillation at very low pressure.
  * The titanium is melted in an electric furnace and poured into moulds.

    Steel is produced at about 8000 tonnes per day. The main steps to make steel are:
  * Iron oxide is reacted with carbon (coke) in a blast furnace that runs continuously.
  * The molten impure iron flows to the bottom of the furnace and is removed every four hours.
  * Oxygen is blown into the molten iron for about 20 minutes to produce steel.
  * The steel is poured into moulds.

    Explain why titanium costs more than steel. (6)

                                                  AQA, 2008

6 Olives are the fruits of the olive tree. Olive oil is extracted from olives.

  a Use a word from the list to complete the sentence.

    condensed   evaporated   pressed

    In the first step to extract the oil the olives are crushed and .... (1)

  b This gives a mixture of liquids and solids that is left to settle.

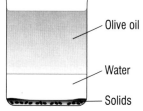

    Why does the olive oil separate from the water? (1)

  c The olive oil is removed from the water and filtered to remove any small pieces of solids.

    Suggest **two** reasons why separating olive oil by this method is better than separating it by distilling. (2)

  d Olive oil can be used as a fuel. Explain why. (2)

  e Food can be cooked in olive oil. Give one advantage and one disadvantage of cooking food in olive oil. (2)

  f Olive oil can be used with vinegar to make salad dressings. Name the type of substance that is added to salad dressings to stop them from separating. (1)

AQA **Examiner's tip**

You may be given information about familiar or unfamiliar applications of chemistry. The information you are given should help you to answer the questions. Q5(b) requires you to organise information clearly. Think about the points in the information and decide which ones make titanium more expensive than steel. Underline or circle the points you are going to use on the question paper. Add brief notes, perhaps numbers for the order that you will use. Think about how you are going to write your answer. Rehearse it in your head before you write your answer.

AQA **Examiner's tip**

Always be aware of the number of marks for a question. If it is two marks, you need to make two points in your answer. Sometimes this is obvious, as in Q6(c), but in Q6(d) you need to make sure you have not given just a single simple statement.

C2 1.2

Ionic bonding ⓚ

Learning objectives

- How are ionic compounds held together?

- Which elements, other than those in Groups 1 and 7, form ions?

You have seen how positive and negative ions form during some reactions. Ionic compounds are usually formed when metals react with non-metals.

The ions formed are held next to each other by very strong forces of attraction between the oppositely charged ions. This electrostatic force of attraction, which acts in all directions, is called **ionic bonding**.

The ionic bonds between the charged particles result in an arrangement of ions that we call a **giant structure** (or a **giant lattice**). If we could stand among the ions they would seem to go on in all directions forever.

The force exerted by an ion on the other ions in the lattice acts equally in all directions. This is why the ions in a giant structure are held so strongly together.

The giant structure of ionic compounds is very regular. This is because the ions all pack together neatly, like marbles in a box.

a What name do we give to the arrangement of ions in an ionic compound?

b What holds the ions together in this structure?

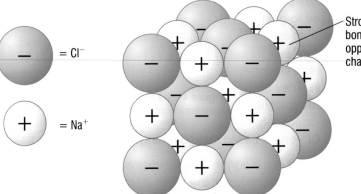

Figure 1 Part of the giant ionic lattice (3-D network) of sodium and chloride ions in sodium chloride

Sometimes the atoms reacting need to gain or lose two electrons to gain a stable noble gas structure. An example is when magnesium (2,8,2) reacts with oxygen (2,6). When these two elements react they form magnesium oxide (MgO). This is made up of magnesium ions with a double positive charge (Mg^{2+}) and oxide ions with a double negative charge (O^{2-}).

We can represent the atoms and ions involved in forming ionic bonds by **dot and cross diagrams**. In these diagrams we only show the electrons in the outermost shell of each atom or ion. This makes them quicker to draw than the diagrams on the previous page. Figure 2 on the next page shows an example.

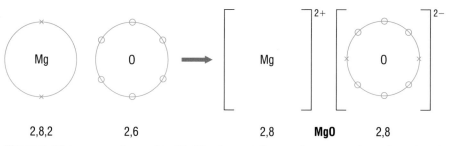

2,8,2   2,6   2,8   **MgO**   2,8

Figure 2 When magnesium oxide (MgO) is formed, the reacting magnesium atoms lose two electrons and the oxygen atoms gain two electrons

Did you know ...?

The structure of ionic lattices is investigated by passing X-rays through them.

Another example of an ionic compound is calcium chloride. Each calcium atom (2,8,8,2) needs to lose two electrons but each chlorine atom (2,8,7) needs to gain only one electron. This means that two chlorine atoms react with every one calcium atom to form calcium chloride. So the formula of calcium chloride is $CaCl_2$.

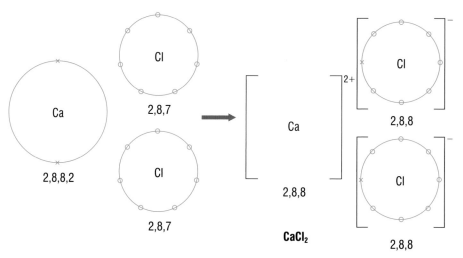

Figure 3 The formation of calcium chloride ($CaCl_2$)

Summary questions

1 **a** Copy and complete the table:

Atomic number	Atom	Electronic structure of atom	Ion	Electronic structure of ion
8	O			$[2,8]^{2-}$
19		2,8,8,1	K^+	
17	Cl		Cl^-	
20		2,8,8,2		

b Explain why potassium chloride is KCl but potassium oxide is K_2O.

c Explain why calcium oxide is CaO but calcium chloride is $CaCl_2$.

2 Draw dot and cross diagrams to show how you would expect the following elements to form ions together:

a lithium and chlorine

b calcium and oxygen

c aluminium and fluorine.

Key points

- Ionic compounds are held together by strong forces of attraction between the oppositely charged ions. This is called ionic bonding.

- Besides the elements in Groups 1 and 7, other elements that can form ionic compounds include those from Groups 2 and 6.

C2 1.3 Formulae of ionic compounds ⓚ

Learning objectives

● How can we write the formula of an ionic compound, given its ions?

In this chapter we have seen how three different ionic compounds are formed. You should understand how atoms turn to ions when sodium chloride, magnesium oxide and calcium chloride are formed from their elements.

The overall charge on any ionic compound is zero. The compounds are neutral. Therefore we do not have to draw dot and cross diagrams to work out each ionic formula. As long as we know or are given the charge on the ions in a compound we can work out its formula.

a What is the overall charge on an ionic compound?

If we look at the three examples above, we can see how the charges on the ions in a compound cancel out:

Ionic compound	Ratio of ions in compound	Formula of compound
sodium chloride	$Na^+ : Cl^-$ 1:1	NaCl
magnesium oxide	$Mg^{2+} : O^{2-}$ 1:1	MgO
calcium chloride	$Ca^{2+} : Cl^-$ 1:2	$CaCl_2$

b What is the formula of magnesium chloride?

We can work out the formula of some ions given a copy of the periodic table. Remember that in your exams you will have a Data Sheet which includes a periodic table and a table showing the charges of common ions.

Groups of metals

● The atoms of Group 1 elements form 1+ ions, e.g. Li^+.
● The atoms of Group 2 elements form 2+ ions, e.g. Ca^{2+}.

Groups of non-metals

● The atoms of Group 7 elements form 1− ions, e.g. F^-.
● The atoms of Group 6 elements form 2− ions, e.g. S^{2-}.

The names of compounds of transition metals contain the charge on their ions in brackets in roman numerals. This is because they can form ions carrying different sizes of positive charge. For example, iron can form 2+ and 3+ ions. So the name iron(III) oxide tells us that the iron is present as Fe^{3+} ions in this compound.

c What is the formula of lithium sulfide?
d What is the formula of iron(III) oxide?

?? Did you know ... ?

Common salt is sodium chloride. In just 58.5 g of salt there are over 600 000 000 000 000 000 000 000 ions of Na^+ and the same number of Cl^- ions.

More complicated ions

Some ions are made up of more than one element. When you studied limestone, you learned that the formula of calcium carbonate is $CaCO_3$. It contains calcium ions, Ca^{2+}, and carbonate ions, CO_3^{2-}. The carbonate ions contain carbon and oxygen. However, the rule about cancelling out charges still applies as in one-element ions. Calcium carbonate is $CaCO_3$ as the 2+ and 2− ions in the ionic compound cancel out in the ratio 1:1.

Two-element ions you might come across are shown in the table below:

Name of ion	Formula of ion	Example of compound
hydroxide	OH^-	calcium hydroxide, $Ca(OH)_2$
nitrate	NO_3^-	magnesium nitrate, $Mg(NO_3)_2$
carbonate	CO_3^{2-}	sodium carbonate, Na_2CO_3
sulfate	SO_4^{2-}	calcium sulfate, $CaSO_4$

Notice how the formula of a compound containing a two-element ion sometimes contains brackets. To write calcium hydroxide as $CaOH_2$ would be misleading. It would tell us the ratio of Ca:O:H ions was 1:1:2. However, as there are twice as many hydroxide ions as calcium ions, the ratio should be 1:2:2. This is why we write the formula as $Ca(OH)_2$.

e What is the formula of calcium nitrate?

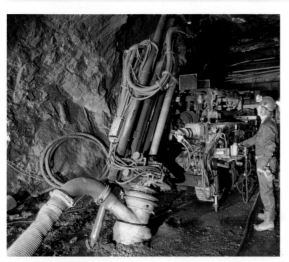

Figure 1 Haematite is an ore of iron. It is mined (as here) and used as a source of iron(III) oxide for the blast furnace in the extraction of iron.

Summary questions

1 Using the charges on the ions given on this spread, give the formula of:
   a calcium oxide
   b lithium oxide
   c magnesium chloride

2 Draw a table with K^+, Mg^{2+} and Fe^{3+} down the side and Br^-, OH^-, NO_3^- and SO_4^{2-} across the top. Then fill in the formula of the compound in each cell of the table.

3 **a** The formula of strontium nitrate is $Sr(NO_3)_2$. What is the charge on a strontium ion?
   b The formula of aluminium sulfate is $Al_2(SO_4)_3$. What is the charge on an aluminium ion?

Key points

- The charges on the ions in an ionic compound always cancel each other out.

- The formula of an ionic compound shows the ratio of ions present in the compound.

- Sometimes we need brackets to show the ratio of ions in a compound, e.g. magnesium hydroxide, $Mg(OH)_2$.

C2 1.4

Covalent bonding

Learning objectives

- How are covalent bonds formed?

- What types of substance have covalent bonds?

Figure 1 Most of the molecules in substances which make up living things are held together by covalent bonds between non-metal atoms

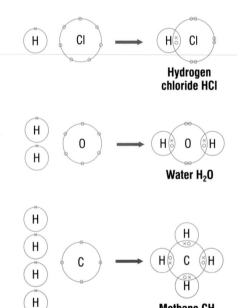

Figure 3 The principles of covalent bonding remain the same however many atoms are involved

Reactions between metals and non-metals usually result in ionic bonding. However, many, many compounds are formed in a very different way. When non-metals react together their atoms share pairs of electrons to form molecules. We call this **covalent bonding**.

Simple molecules

The atoms of non-metals generally need to gain electrons to achieve stable outer energy levels. When they react together neither atom can give away electrons. So they get the electronic structure of a noble gas by sharing electrons. The atoms in the molecules are then held together by the shared pairs of electrons. We call these strong bonds between the atoms covalent bonds.

a What is the bond called when two atoms share a pair of electrons?

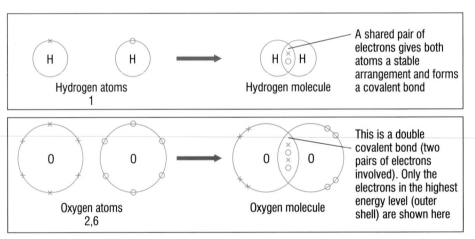

Figure 2 Atoms of hydrogen and oxygen join together to form stable molecules. The atoms in H_2 and O_2 molecules are held together by strong covalent bonds.

Sometimes in covalent bonding each atom brings the same number of electrons to share. But this is not always the case. Sometimes the atoms of one element will need several electrons, while the other element only needs one more electron for each atom to get a stable arrangement. In this case, more atoms become involved in forming the molecule.

We can represent the covalent bonds in substances such as water, ammonia and methane in a number of ways. Each way represents the same thing. The method chosen depends on what we want to show.

Figure 4 We can represent a covalent compound by showing **a** the highest energy levels (or outer shells), **b** the outer electrons in a dot and cross diagram or **c** the number of covalent bonds

Giant covalent structures

Many substances containing covalent bonds consist of small molecules, for example, H_2O. However, some covalently bonded substances are very different. They have giant structures where huge numbers of atoms are held together by a network of covalent bonds. These are sometimes referred to as macromolecules.

Diamond has a giant covalent structure. In diamond, each carbon atom forms four covalent bonds with its neighbours. This results in a rigid giant covalent lattice.

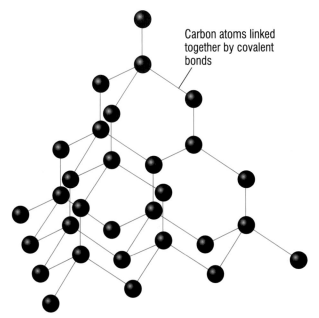

Carbon atoms linked together by covalent bonds

Figure 5 Part of the giant covalent structure of diamond

Figure 6 Diamonds owe their hardness to the way the carbon atoms are arranged in a giant covalent structure

Silicon dioxide (silica) is another substance with a giant covalent structure.

b What do we call the structure of a substance held together by a network of covalent bonds?

Summary questions

1 Copy and complete using the words below:

covalent   giant   molecules   macromolecules   shared

When non-metal atoms react together they make .... bonds. The atoms in these bonds are held together by .... electrons. Most substances held together by covalent bonds consist of ...., but some have .... covalent structures, sometimes called ....

2 Draw diagrams, showing all the electrons, to represent the covalent bonding between the following atoms.
  a two hydrogen atoms
  b two chlorine atoms
  c a hydrogen atom and a fluorine atom

3 Draw dot and cross diagrams to show the covalent bonds when:
  a a nitrogen atom bonds with three hydrogen atoms
  b a carbon atom bonds with two oxygen atoms.

Key points

● Covalent bonds are formed when atoms share pairs of electrons.

● Many substances containing covalent bonds consist of simple molecules, but some have giant covalent structures.

Summary questions ⓚ

1 Define the following terms:

compound
ionic bonding
covalent bond

2 a Which of the following substances will have ionic bonding?

hydrogen sulfide   copper   phosphorus(v) oxide
iron(II) chloride   potassium oxide   lead bromide
silver nitrate

b Explain how you decided on your answers in part **a**.

c What type of bonding will the remaining substances in the list have?

d What is the formula of:

i hydrogen sulfide
ii iron(II) chloride.

e Why does iron(II) chloride have roman numerals in its name?

3 Copy and complete the following table with the formula of each compound formed.

(The first one is done for you).

	fluoride, F^-	oxide, O^{2-}	carbonate, CO_3^{2-}	phosphate(V), PO_4^{3-}
lithium, Li^+	LiF			
barium, Ba^{2+}				
copper, Cu^{2+}				
aluminium, Al^{3+}				

4 a Which of the following substances are made up of small molecules and which have a giant covalent structure?

methane, CH_4
silicon dioxide, SiO_2
diamond, C
ammonia, NH_3

b Draw a dot and cross diagram to show the bonding in ammonia.

5 The diagrams show the arrangement of electrons in energy levels in three atoms:

(The letters are NOT the chemical symbols.)

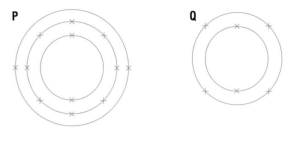

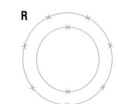

a Which atom belongs to Group 2 of the periodic table?

b To which group does atom R belong?

c i Atom Q bonds with four atoms of hydrogen. Draw a dot and cross diagram to show the compound that is formed.

ii What do we call the type of bonding between the atom of Q and the hydrogen atoms?

d i Draw dot and cross diagrams to show how atom P bonds with R atoms.

ii What do we call the type of bonding in the compound formed by P and R?

iii What is the formula of the compound formed by P and R?

6 Describe, with diagrams, how the particles are held together in the following substances:

a a molecule of fluorine (F_2)

b a salt crystal (NaCl).

7 Draw a diagram which shows how the atoms in carbon dioxide, O=C=O, bond to each other.   [H]

AQA Examination-style questions ⓚ

Use a periodic table and a table of charges on ions to help you to answer these questions.

1 Choose a word from the list to complete each sentence.
   a When metals react with non-metals electrons
   are ....   (1)

   combined   shared   transferred

   b When non-metal elements combine their atoms are
   held together by .... bonds.   (1)

   covalent   ionic   metallic

2 Choose a description from the list for each of the
substances.

   giant covalent   giant ionic   metal   simple molecule

   a ammonia, NH_3 **c** lithium, Li

   b diamond, C   **d** sodium oxide, Na_2O (4)

3 Choose a number from the list to complete each
sentence.

   0   1   2   3   4   6   7

   a The elements in Group .... in the periodic table all
   form ions with a charge of 1+.   (1)
   b The elements in Group .... in the periodic table all
   form ions with a charge of 2−.   (1)
   c The elements in Group 4 in the periodic table all form
   .... covalent bonds.   (1)
   d The aluminium ion has a charge of .... +   (1)

4 a Choose the correct formula from the list for iron(III)
   chloride.

   FeCl Fe_3Cl $FeCl_3$ Fe_3Cl_3   (1)

   b Choose the formula from the list for each of these ionic
   compounds.

   NaS $NaSO_4$ $Na(SO_4)_2$ Na_2S NaS_2 Na_2SO_4

   i sodium sulfide   (1)
   ii sodium sulfate   (1)

5 Calcium hydroxide, $Ca(OH)_2$, is an ionic compound.

   Which of these ions in the list are the ions in calcium
   hydroxide?

   Ca^+ Ca^{2+} Ca^{4+} OH^- OH_2^- OH^{2-} (2)

6 Sodium reacts with chlorine. The reaction forms
sodium chloride.

   a Use words from the list to answer the questions.

   compound   element   hydrocarbon   mixture

   Which word best describes:
   i sodium   (1)
   ii sodium chloride?   (1)

b When sodium reacts with chlorine the sodium atoms
change into sodium ions. The diagrams represent a
sodium atom and a sodium ion.

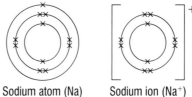

Sodium atom (Na)   Sodium ion (Na⁺)

Use the diagrams to help you explain how a sodium
atom turns into a sodium ion.   (2)

c i The diagram below represents a chlorine atom.
When chlorine reacts with sodium the chlorine
forms negative chloride ions.
Copy and complete the diagram below to show
how the outer electrons are arranged in a chloride
ion (Cl⁻).   (1)

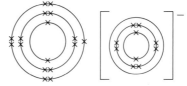

   ii Chloride ions are strongly attracted to sodium ions
   in sodium chloride.

   Explain why.   (1)
                                                                   AQA, 2010

7 Chlorine can form compounds with ionic or covalent
bonds.

   a Potassium chloride, KCl, has ionic bonds. Draw
   dot and cross diagrams to show what happens to
   potassium atoms and chlorine atoms when they react
   to form potassium chloride. You only need to show the
   outer electrons in your diagrams.   (4)

   b Hydrogen chloride, HCl, has covalent bonds. Draw
   a dot and cross diagram to show the bonding in
   hydrogen chloride.   (2)

8 Sodium metal is a giant structure of sodium atoms.

   Explain how the atoms are held together in sodium
   metal.   [H] (3)

C2 2.4 Giant metallic structures ⓚ

Learning objectives

- Why can we bend and shape metals?
- Why are alloys harder than pure metals?
- Why do metals allow electricity and heat to pass through them? [H]
- What are shape memory alloys?

Figure 1 Drawing copper out into wires depends on being able to make the layers of metal atoms slide easily over each other

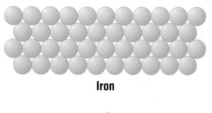

Iron

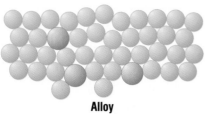

Alloy

Figure 2 The atoms in pure iron are arranged in layers which can easily slide over each other. In alloys the layers cannot slide so easily because atoms of other elements change the regular structure.

We can hammer and bend metals into different shapes, and draw them out into wires. This is because the layers of atoms in a pure metal are able to slide easily over each other.

The atoms in a pure metal, such as iron, are held together in giant metallic structures. The atoms are arranged in closely-packed layers. Because of this regular arrangement, the atoms can slide over one another quite easily. This is why pure iron is soft and easily shaped.

a Why can metals be bent, shaped and pulled out into wires when forces are applied?

Alloys are usually mixtures of metals. However, most steels contain iron with controlled amounts of carbon, a non-metal, mixed in its structure. So there are different sizes of atoms in an alloy. This makes it more difficult for the layers in the metal's giant structure to slide over each other. So alloys are harder than the pure metals used to make them. This is shown in Figure 2.

Practical

Making models of metals

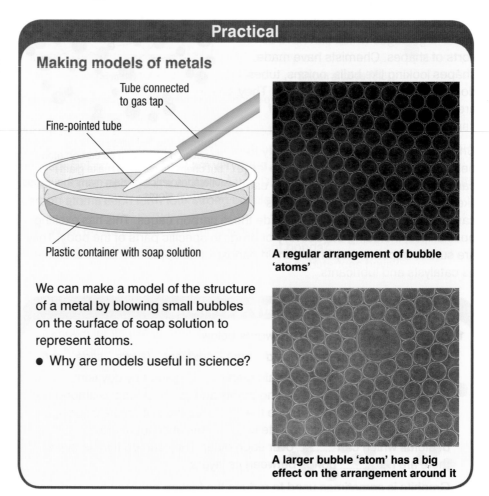

A regular arrangement of bubble 'atoms'

A larger bubble 'atom' has a big effect on the arrangement around it

We can make a model of the structure of a metal by blowing small bubbles on the surface of soap solution to represent atoms.

- Why are models useful in science?

Metal cooking utensils are used all over the world, because metals are good conductors of heat. Wherever we generate electricity, it passes through metal wires to where it is needed. That's because metals are also good conductors of electricity.

Higher

Explaining the properties of metals

The positive ions in a metal's giant structure are held together by a sea of delocalised electrons. These electrons are a bit like 'glue'. Their negative charge between the positively charged ions holds the ions in position.

However, unlike glue, the electrons are able to move throughout the whole giant lattice. Because they can move around and hold the metal ions together at the same time, the delocalised electrons enable the lattice to distort. When struck, the metal atoms can slip past one another without breaking up the metal's structure.

b How are metal atoms held together?

Metals are good conductors of heat and electricity because the delocalised electrons can flow through the giant metallic lattice. The electrical current and heat are transferred quickly through the metal by the free electrons.

c Why do metals conduct electricity and heat so well?

Figure 3 Metals are essential in our lives – the delocalised electrons mean that they are good conductors of both heat and electricity

Shape memory alloys

Some alloys have a very special property. Like all metals they can be bent (or **deformed**) into different shapes. The difference comes when you heat them up. They then return to their original shape all by themselves.

We call these metals **shape memory alloys**, which describes the way they behave. They seem to 'remember' their original shape!

We can use the properties of shape memory alloys in many ways, for example in health care. Doctors treating a badly broken bone can use alloys to hold the bones in place while they heal. They cool the alloy before it is wrapped around the broken bone. When it heats up again the alloy goes back to its original shape. This pulls the bones together and holds them while they heal.

Dentists have also made braces to pull teeth into the right position using this technique.

⊙⊙ links

For more about the bonding in metals, look back at C2 1.5 Metals.

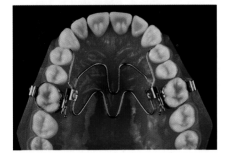

Figure 4 This dental brace pulls the teeth into the right position as it warms up. It is made of a shape memory alloy called nitinol. It is an alloy of nickel and titanium.

Summary questions

1 Copy and complete using the words below:

delocalised   electricity   energy   heat   shape   slide

The positively charged .... in metals are held together by .... electrons. These also allow the layers to .... over each other so that the metal's .... can be changed. They also allow the metal to conduct .... and .... **[H]**

2 a Use your knowledge of metal structures to explain how adding larger metal atoms to a metallic lattice can make the metal harder.
   b What is a shape memory alloy?

3 Explain how a dental brace made out of nitinol is more effective than a brace made out of a traditional alloy.

4 Explain why metals are good conductors of heat and electricity. **[H]**

Key points

- We can bend and shape metals because the layers of atoms (or ions) in a giant metallic structure can slide over each other.

- Delocalised electrons in metals enable electricity and heat to pass through the metal easily. **[H]**

- If a shape memory alloy is deformed, it can return to its original shape on heating.

C2 3.3

Percentages and formulae

Learning objectives

- How can we calculate the percentage of an element in a compound from its formula?

- How can we calculate the empirical formula of a compound from its percentage composition? [H]

Figure 1 A small difference in the amount of metal in an ore might not seem very much. However, when millions of tonnes of ore are extracted and processed each year, it all adds up!

Maths skills

To calculate the percentage of an element in a compound:

- Write down the formula of the compound.

- Using the A_r values from your data sheet, work out the M_r of the compound. Write down the mass of each element making up the compound as you work it out.

- Write the mass of the element you are investigating as a fraction of the M_r.

- Find the percentage by multiplying your fraction by 100.

We can use the formula mass of a compound to calculate the percentage mass of each element in it. It's not just in GCSE Chemistry books that calculations like this are done! Mining companies decide whether to exploit mineral finds using calculations like these.

Working out the percentage of an element in a compound

Worked example 1

What percentage of the mass of magnesium oxide is actually magnesium?

Solution

We need to know the formula of magnesium oxide: MgO.

The A_r of magnesium is 24 and the A_r of oxygen is 16.

Adding these together gives us the relative formula mass (M_r), of MgO
$24 + 16 = 40$

So in 40 g of magnesium oxide, 24 g is actually magnesium.

The fraction of magnesium in the MgO is:

$$\frac{\text{mass of magnesium}}{\text{total mass of compound}} = \frac{24}{40}$$

so the percentage of magnesium in the compound is:

$$\frac{24}{40} \times 100\% = \mathbf{60\%}$$

Worked example 2

A pure white powder is found at the scene of a crime. It could be strychnine, a deadly poison with the formula $C_{21}H_{22}N_2O_2$: but is it?

When a chemist analyses the powder, she finds that 83% of its mass is carbon. What is the percentage mass of carbon in strychnine? Is this the same as the white powder?

Solution

Given the A_r values: C = 12, H = 1, N = 14, O = 16, the formula mass (M_r) of strychnine is:

$(12 \times 21) + (1 \times 22) + (14 \times 2) + (16 \times 2) = 252 + 22 + 28 + 32 = 334$

The percentage mass of carbon in strychnine is therefore:

$$\frac{252}{334} \times 100 = \mathbf{75.4\%}$$

This is **not** the same as the percentage mass of carbon in the white powder – so the white powder is not strychnine.

a What is the percentage mass of hydrogen in ammonia, NH_3? (A_r values: N = 14, H = 1)

Higher

Working out the empirical formula of a compound from its percentage composition (k)

We can find the percentage of each element in a compound by experiments. Then we can work out the simplest ratio of each type of atom in the compound. We call this simplest (whole-number) ratio its **empirical formula**.

This is sometimes the same as the actual number of atoms in one molecule (which we call the **molecular formula**) – but not always. For example, the empirical formula of water is H_2O, which is also its molecular formula. However, hydrogen peroxide has the empirical formula HO, but its molecular formula is H_2O_2.

Worked example

A hydrocarbon contains 75% carbon and 25% hydrogen by mass. What is its empirical formula? (A_r values: C = 12, H = 1)

Solution

Imagine we have 100 g of the compound. Then 75 g is carbon and 25 g hydrogen.

Work out the number of moles by dividing the mass of each element by its relative atomic mass:

$$\text{For carbon: } \frac{75}{12} = 6.25 \text{ moles of carbon atoms}$$

For hydrogen: $\frac{25}{1} = 25$ moles of hydrogen atoms

So this tells us that 6.25 moles of carbon atoms are combined with 25 moles of hydrogen atoms.

This means that the ratio is 6.25 (C) : 25 (H).

So the simplest whole number ratio is 1 : 4 (by dividing both numbers by the smallest number in the ratio)

In other words each carbon atom is combined with 4 times as many hydrogen atoms.

So the empirical formula is **CH_4**.

> **b** A compound contains 40% sulfur and 60% oxygen. What is its empirical formula? (A_r values: S = 32, O = 16)
>
> **c** 5.4 g of aluminium react exactly with 4.8 g of oxygen. What is the empirical formula of the compound formed? (A_r values: Al = 27, O = 16)

Maths skills

To work out the formula from percentage masses:

● Change the percentages given to the masses of each element in 100 g of compound.

● Change the masses to moles of atoms by dividing the masses by the A_r values. This tells you how many moles of each different element are present.

● This tells you the ratio of atoms of the different elements in the compound.

● Then the *simplest* whole-number ratio gives you the empirical formula of the compound. [H]

Summary questions

1 Copy and complete using the words below:

compound   dividing   hundred   formula

The percentage of an element in a .... is calculated by .... the mass of the element in the compound by the relative .... mass of the compound and then multiplying the result by one ....

2 Ammonium nitrate (NH_4NO_3) is used as a fertiliser. What is the percentage mass of nitrogen in it? (A_r values: H = 1, N = 14, O = 16)

3 22.55% of the mass of a sample of phosphorus chloride is phosphorus. What is the empirical formula of this phosphorus chloride? (A_r values: P = 31, Cl = 35.5) [H]

Key points

● The relative atomic masses of the elements in a compound and its formula can be used to work out its percentage composition.

● We can calculate empirical formulae given the masses or percentage composition of elements present. [H]

C2 3.4

Equations and calculations ⓚ

Learning objectives

- What do balanced symbol equations tell us about chemical reactions?

- How do we use balanced symbol equations to calculate masses of reactants and products? [H]

Chemical equations can be very useful. When we want to know how much of each substance is involved in a chemical reaction, we can use the balanced symbol equation.

Think about what happens when hydrogen molecules (H_2) react with chlorine molecules (Cl_2). The reaction makes hydrogen chloride molecules (HCl):

$$H_2 + Cl_2 \rightarrow HCl \text{ (not balanced)}$$

This equation shows the reactants and the product – but it is not balanced.

Here is the balanced equation:

$$H_2 + Cl_2 \rightarrow 2HCl$$

This balanced equation tells us that '1 hydrogen molecule reacts with 1 chlorine molecule to make 2 hydrogen chloride molecules'. But the balanced equation also tells us the number of moles of each substance involved. So our balanced equation also tells us that '1 mole of hydrogen molecules reacts with 1 mole of chlorine molecules to make 2 moles of hydrogen chloride molecules'.

a '2HCl' has two meanings. What are they?

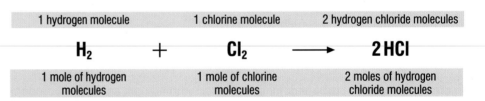

1 hydrogen molecule	1 chlorine molecule	2 hydrogen chloride molecules
H_2 +	Cl_2 ⟶	2 HCl
1 mole of hydrogen molecules	1 mole of chlorine molecules	2 moles of hydrogen chloride molecules

Using balanced equations to work out reacting masses

This balanced equation above is really useful, because we can use it to work out what mass of hydrogen and chlorine react together. We can also calculate how much hydrogen chloride is made.

To do this, we need to know that the A_r for hydrogen is 1 and the A_r for chlorine is 35.5:

A_r of hydrogen = 1 .... so mass of 1 mole of H_2 = 2 × 1 = 2 g

A_r of chlorine = 35.5 .... so mass of 1 mole of Cl_2 = 2 × 35.5 = 71 g

M_r of HCl = (1 + 35.5) = 36.5 .... so mass of 1 mole of HCl = 36.5 g

Our balanced equation tells us that 1 mole of hydrogen reacts with 1 mole of chlorine to give 2 moles of HCl. So turning this into masses we get:

1 mole of hydrogen = 1 × 2 g = 2 g

1 mole of chlorine = 1 × 71 g = 71 g

2 moles of HCl = 2 × 36.5 g = 73 g

Higher

Higher

Calculations (k)

These calculations are important when we want to know the mass of chemicals that react together. For example, sodium hydroxide reacts with chlorine gas to make bleach.

Here is the balanced symbol equation for the reaction:

$$2NaOH \quad + \quad Cl_2 \quad \rightarrow NaOCl + NaCl + H_2O$$
sodium hydroxide   chlorine   bleach   salt   water

This reaction happens when chlorine gas is bubbled through a solution of sodium hydroxide.

If we have a solution containing 100 g of sodium hydroxide, how much chlorine gas do we need to convert it to **bleach**? Too much, and some chlorine will be wasted. Too little, and not all of the sodium hydroxide will react.

	Mass of 1 mole of	
	NaOH	**Cl₂**
A_r of hydrogen = 1		
A_r of oxygen = 16	= 23 + 16 + 1 = 40	= 35.5 × 2 = 71
A_r of sodium = 23		
A_r of chlorine = 35.5		

The table shows that 1 mole of sodium hydroxide has a mass of 40 g.

So 100 g of sodium hydroxide is $\frac{100}{40}$ = 2.5 moles.

The balanced symbol equation tells us that for every 2 moles of sodium hydroxide we need 1 mole of chlorine.

So we need $\frac{2.5}{2}$ = 1.25 moles of chlorine.

The table shows that 1 mole of chlorine has a mass of 71 g.

So we will need 1.25 × 71 = **88.75 g** of chlorine to react with 100 g of sodium hydroxide.

Figure 1 Bleach is used in some swimming pools to kill harmful bacteria. Getting the quantities right involves some careful calculation!

Summary questions

1 Copy and complete using the words below:

balanced   equations   mole   mass   product

Symbol .... can tell us about the amounts of substances in a reaction if they are .... To work out the mass of each substance in a reaction we need to know the mass of 1 .... of it. We can then work out the .... of each reactant needed, and the mass of .... that will be formed.   [H]

2 a Hydrogen peroxide, H_2O_2, decomposes to form water and oxygen gas. Write a balanced symbol equation for this reaction.

b When hydrogen peroxide decomposes, what mass of hydrogen peroxide is needed to produce 8 g of oxygen gas?
(A_r values: H = 1, O = 16)   [H]

3 Calcium reacts with oxygen like this:

$$2Ca + O_2 \rightarrow 2CaO$$

What mass of oxygen will react exactly with 60 g of calcium?
(A_r values: O = 16, Ca = 40)   [H]

Key points

- Balanced symbol equations tell us the number of moles of substances involved in a chemical reaction.

- We can use balanced symbol equations to calculate the masses of reactants and products in a chemical reaction.   [H]

C2 3.5

The yield of a chemical reaction

Learning objectives

- What do we mean by the yield of a chemical reaction and what factors affect it?
- How do we calculate the percentage yield of a chemical reaction?   [H]
- Why is it important to achieve a high yield in industry and to waste as little energy as possible?

⬭ links

For information about using balanced symbol equations to predict reacting masses, look back to C2 3.4 Equations and calculations.

Many of the substances that we use every day have to be made from other chemicals. This may involve using complex chemical reactions. Examples include food colourings, flavourings and preservatives, the ink in your pen or printer, and the artificial fibres in your clothes. All of these are made using chemical reactions.

Imagine a reaction: $A + 2B \rightarrow C$

If we need 1000 kg of C, we can work out how much A and B we need. All we need to know is the relative formula masses of A, B and C and the balanced symbol equation.

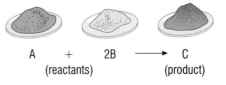

A + 2B ⟶ C
(reactants)   (product)

> a How many moles of B are needed to react with each mole of A in this reaction?
> b How many moles of C will this make?

If we carry out the reaction, it is unlikely that we will get as much of C as we worked out. This is because our calculations assumed that all of A and B would be turned into C. We call the amount of product that a chemical reaction produces its **yield**.

It is useful to think about reactions in terms of their **percentage yield**. This compares the amount of product that the reaction *really* produces with the maximum amount that it could *possibly* produce:

$$\text{Percentage yield} = \frac{\text{amount of product produced}}{\text{maxmimum amount of product possible}} \times 100\%$$

Calculating percentage yield

An industrial example

Limestone is made mainly of calcium carbonate. Crushed lumps of limestone are heated in a rotating lime kiln. The calcium carbonate decomposes to make calcium oxide, and carbon dioxide gas is given off. A company processes 200 tonnes of limestone a day. It collects 98 tonnes of calcium oxide, the useful product. What is the percentage yield of the kiln, assuming limestone contains only calcium carbonate?

(A_r values: Ca = 40, C = 12, O = 16)

calcium carbonate → calcium oxide + carbon dioxide

$$CaCO_3 \quad \rightarrow \quad CaO \quad + \quad CO_2$$

Work out the relative formula masses of $CaCO_3$ and CaO.

M_r of $CaCO_3$ = 40 + 12 + (16 × 3) = 100

M_r of CaO = 40 + 16 = 56

So the balanced symbol equation tells us that:

100 tonnes of $CaCO_3$ could make 56 tonnes of CaO, assuming a 100% yield.

Higher

Higher

Therefore 200 tonnes of $CaCO_3$ could make a maximum of (56×2) tonnes of $CaO = 112$ tonnes.

So **percentage yield** $= \dfrac{\textbf{amount of product produced}}{\textbf{maximum amount of product possible}} \times \textbf{100\%}$

$= \dfrac{98}{112} \times 100 = \textbf{87.5\%}$

We can explain this yield as some of the limestone is lost as dust in the crushing process and in the rotating kiln. There will also be some other mineral compounds in the limestone. It is not 100% calcium carbonate as we assumed in our calculation.

c What is the percentage yield of a reaction?

Very few chemical reactions have a yield of 100% because:

- The reaction may be reversible (so as products form they react to re-form the reactants again).
- Some reactants may react to give unexpected products.
- Some of the product may be lost in handling or left behind in the apparatus.
- The reactants may not be completely pure.
- Some chemical reactions produce more than one product, and it may be difficult to separate the product that we want from the reaction mixture.

Sustainable production

Chemical companies use reactions to make products which they sell. Ideally, they want to use reactions with high yields (that also happen at a reasonable rate). Making a product more efficiently means making less waste. As much product as possible should be made from the reactants.

Chemical factories (or **plants**) are designed by chemical engineers. They design a plant to work as safely and economically as possible. It should waste as little energy and raw materials as possible. This helps the company to make money. It is better for the environment too as it conserves our limited resources. It also reduces the pollution we get when we use fossil fuels as sources of energy.

Summary questions

1 Copy and complete using the words below:

high   maximum   percentage   product   waste   yield

The amount of .... made in a chemical reaction is called its .... The .... yield tells us the amount of product that is made compared to the .... amount that could be made. Reactions with .... yields are important because they result in less ....

2 Explain why it is good for the environment if industry finds ways to make products using high yield reactions and processes that waste as little energy as possible.

3 If the percentage yield for a reaction is 100%, 60 g of reactant A would make 80 g of product C. How much of reactant A is needed to make 80 g of product C if the percentage yield of the reaction is only 75%?   **[H]**

Key points

- The yield of a chemical reaction describes how much product is made.
- The percentage yield of a chemical reaction tells us how much product is made compared with the maximum amount that could be made (100%).
- Factors affecting the yield of a chemical reaction include product being left behind in the apparatus and difficulty separating the products from the reaction mixture.
- It is important to maximise yield and minimise energy wasted to conserve the Earth's limited resources and reduce pollution.

C2 3.6 Reversible reactions

Learning objectives

- What is a reversible reaction?
- How can we represent reversible reactions?

Figure 1 Indicators undergo reversible reactions, changing colour to show us whether solutions are acidic or alkaline

In all the reactions we have looked at so far the reactants react and form products. We show this by using an arrow pointing *from* the reactants *to* the products:

$$A + B \rightarrow C + D$$
$$\text{reactants} \qquad \text{products}$$

But in some reactions the products can react together to make the original reactants again. We call this a **reversible reaction**.

A reversible reaction can go in both directions so we use two arrows in the equation. One arrow points in the forwards direction and one backwards:

$$A + B \rightleftharpoons C + D$$

a What does a single arrow in a chemical equation mean?
b What does a double arrow in a chemical equation mean?

Examples of reversible reactions

Have you ever tried to neutralise an alkaline solution with an acid? It is very difficult to get a solution which is exactly neutral. You can use an indicator to tell when just the right amount of acid has been added. Indicators react in acids to form a coloured compound. They also react in alkalis to form a differently coloured compound.

Litmus is a complex molecule. We will represent it as HLit (where H is hydrogen). HLit is red. If you add alkali, HLit turns into the Lit$^-$ ion by losing an H$^+$ ion. Lit$^-$ is blue. If you then add more acid, blue Lit$^-$ changes back to red HLit and so on.

$$\underset{\text{Red litmus}}{HLit} \rightleftharpoons \underset{\text{Blue litmus}}{H^+ + Lit^-}$$

c Why does a neutral solution look purple with litmus solution?

Practical

Changing colours

Use litmus solution, dilute hydrochloric acid and sodium hydroxide solution to show the reversible reaction described above.

- Explain the changes you see when adding acid and alkali to litmus.

When we heat ammonium chloride another reversible reaction takes place.

Practical

Heating ammonium chloride

Gently heat a small amount of ammonium chloride in a test tube with a mineral wool plug. Use test tube holders or clamp the test tube at an angle. Make sure you warm the bottom of the tube.

- What do you see happen inside the test tube?

Safety: Wear eye protection for both practicals.

Ammonium chloride breaks down on heating. It forms ammonia gas and hydrogen chloride gas. This is an example of thermal decomposition:

$$\text{ammonium chloride} \xrightarrow{\text{heat}} \text{ammonia} + \text{hydrogen chloride}$$
$$NH_4Cl \xrightarrow{\hspace{2cm}} NH_3 + HCl$$

The two gases rise up the test tube. When they cool down near the mouth of the tube they react with each other. The gases re-form ammonium chloride again. The white solid forms on the inside of the glass:

$$\text{ammonia} + \text{hydrogen chloride} \rightarrow \text{ammonium chloride}$$
$$NH_3 + HCl \rightarrow NH_4Cl$$

We can show the reversible reactions as:

$$\text{ammonium chloride} \rightleftharpoons \text{ammonia} + \text{hydrogen chloride}$$
$$NH_4Cl \rightleftharpoons NH_3 + HCl$$

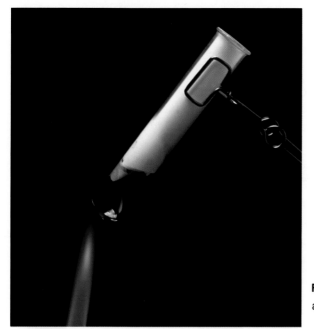

Figure 2 An example of a reversible reaction:
ammonium chloride $\rightleftharpoons$ ammonia + hydrogen chloride
$$NH_4Cl \rightleftharpoons NH_3 + HCl$$

Summary questions

1 What do we mean by 'a *reversible* chemical reaction'?

2 Phenolphthalein is an indicator. It is colourless in acid and pure water but is pink-purple in alkali. In a demonstration a teacher started with a beaker containing a mixture of water and phenolphthalein. In two other beakers she had different volumes of acid and alkali. The acid and alkali had the same concentration.

She then poured the mixture into the beaker containing $2\,cm^3$ of sodium hydroxide solution. Finally she poured the mixture into a third beaker with $5\,cm^3$ of hydrochloric acid in it.

Describe what you would observe happen in the demonstration.

3 We can represent the phenolphthalein indicator as HPhe. Assuming it behaves like litmus, write a symbol equation to show its reversible reaction in acid and alkali. Show the colour of HPhe and Phe⁻ under their formulae in your equation.

Key points

● In a reversible reaction the products of the reaction can react to make the original reactants.

● We can show a reversible reaction using the $\rightleftharpoons$ sign.

Analysing substances

Learning objectives

- What are food additives and how can we identify them?

- How can we detect artificial food colourings?

- What are the advantages of instrumental methods of analysis?

Figure 1 Modern foods contain a variety of additives to improve their taste or appearance, and to make them keep longer

⚬⚬ links

For more information on how chemists identify unknown substances, see C3 4.5 Chemical analysis.

Figure 3 A few years ago a batch of red food colouring was found to be contaminated with a chemical suspected of causing cancer. This dye had found its way into hundreds of processed foods. All of these had to be removed from the shelves of our supermarkets and destroyed.

For hundreds of years we have added salt to food to preserve it. Nowadays, food technologists develop ways to improve the quality of foods. They also analyse foods to ensure they meet legal safety standards.

We call a substance that is added to food to extend its shelf life or to improve its taste or appearance a food additive. Additives that have been approved for use in Europe are given E numbers. The E numbers are like a code to identify the additives. For example, E102 is a yellow food colouring called tartrazine.

a What is a food additive?

Detecting additives

Scientists have many instruments that they can use to identify unknown compounds, including food additives. Many of these are more sensitive, automated versions of techniques we use in school labs.

One technique that is used to identify food additives is paper **chromatography**. It works because some compounds in a mixture dissolve better than others in particular solvents. Their solubility determines how far they travel across the paper.

Practical

Detecting dyes in food colourings

Make a chromatogram to analyse various food colourings.

- What can you deduce from your chromatogram?

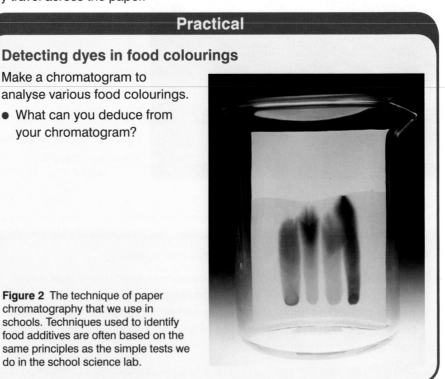

Figure 2 The technique of paper chromatography that we use in schools. Techniques used to identify food additives are often based on the same principles as the simple tests we do in the school science lab.

b What happens to the food colourings when you make a paper chromatogram?

Once the compounds in a food have been separated using chromatography, they can be identified. We can compare the chromatogram with others obtained from known substances. For this we must use the same solvent at the same temperature.

Instrumental methods

Many industries need rapid and accurate methods for analysing their products. They use modern instrumental analysis for this task.

Instrumental techniques are also important in fighting pollution. Careful monitoring of the environment using sensitive instruments is now common. This type of analysis is also used all the time in health care.

Modern instrumental methods have a number of benefits over older methods:

- they are highly accurate and sensitive
- they are quicker
- they enable very small samples to be analysed.

Against this, the main disadvantages of using instrumental methods are that the equipment:

- is usually very expensive
- takes special training to use
- gives results that can often be interpreted only by comparison with data from known substances.

c What do you think has aided the development of instrumental methods of chemical analysis?

d Why are these methods important?

Figure 4 Compared with the methods of 50 years ago, modern instrumental methods of analysis are quick, accurate and sensitive – three big advantages. They also need far fewer people to carry out the analysis than traditional laboratory analysis.

∞ links

For more information on the instruments used by chemists to analyse substances, see C2 3.8 Instrumental analysis.

AQA Examiner's tip

Although simpler to use than bench chemistry methods, instrumental methods still need trained technicians to operate them.

Summary questions

1 Copy and complete using the words below:

additives   paper   analyse   identify

Food scientists can .... different foods to see what .... have been used. For example, food colourings can be detected by .... chromatography. They can use results from known compounds to positively .... them.

2 a Carry out a survey of some processed foods. Identify some examples of food additives and explain why they have been used.

  b Describe how we can separate the dyes in a food colouring and identify them.

3 What are the main advantages and disadvantages of using instrumental analysis compared with traditional practical methods?

Key points

- Additives may be added to food in order to improve its appearance, taste and how long it will keep (its shelf life).

- Food scientists can analyse foods to identify additives, e.g. by using paper chromatography.

- Modern instrumental techniques provide fast, accurate and sensitive ways of analysing chemical substances.

C2 3.8

Instrumental analysis

Learning objectives

- How can we use gas chromatography to separate compounds in a sample mixture?

- How can we use a mass spectrometer to identify the compounds in the sample?

Analysing mixtures

Samples to be analysed are often mixtures of different compounds. So the first step is to separate the compounds. Then they can be identified using one of the many instrumental techniques available. Chemists have developed a technique called gas chromatography–mass spectrometry (GC–MS) to do this task.

- Firstly, they use **gas chromatography** to separate compounds that are easily vaporised.

- Then the separated compounds pass into another instrument – the **mass spectrometer**, which can identify each of them. The mass spectrometer is useful for identifying both elements and compounds. The pattern of peaks it produces identifies the sample.

Gas chromatography

This separation technique is similar to paper chromatography. However, instead of a solvent moving over paper, it has a gas moving through a column packed with a solid.

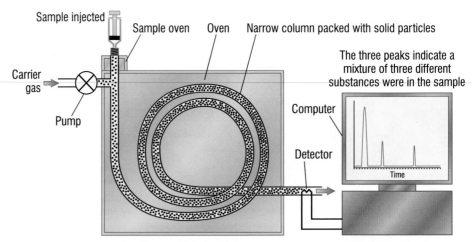

Figure 1 This is the apparatus used in gas chromatography. The solid in the column can be coated in a liquid and is sometimes then known as gas–liquid chromatography.

- First of all, the sample mixture is vaporised.
- A 'carrier' gas moves the vapour through the coiled column.
- The compounds in the sample have different attractions to the material in the column. The compounds with stronger attractions will take longer to get through the column. We say that they have a longer **retention time**.
- The compounds with weak attractions to the material in the column leave it first. They have shorter retention times.

The separated compounds can be recorded on a chart as they leave the column. Look at Figure 2 to see a gas chromatograph.

We can identify the unknown substances in the sample by comparing the chromatograph with the results for known substances. The analysis must have taken place in exactly the same conditions to compare retention times.

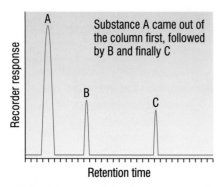

Figure 2 This is a gas chromatograph of a mixture of three different substances. There was more of substance A than B or C in the sample mixture.

Mass spectrometry

To ensure that we identify the unknown substances the gas chromatography apparatus can be attached directly to a **mass spectrometer.** This identifies substances very quickly and accurately and can detect very small quantities in the sample.

Measuring relative molecular masses

A mass spectrometer also provides an accurate way of measuring the relative molecular (formula) mass of a compound. The peak with the largest mass corresponds to an ion with just one electron removed. As you know, the mass of an electron is so small that it can be ignored when we look at the mass of atoms. This peak is called the **molecular ion peak**. It is always found as the last peak on the right as you look at a mass spectrum. The molecular ion peak of the substance analysed in Figure 3 is at 45. So the substance has a relative molecular mass of 45.

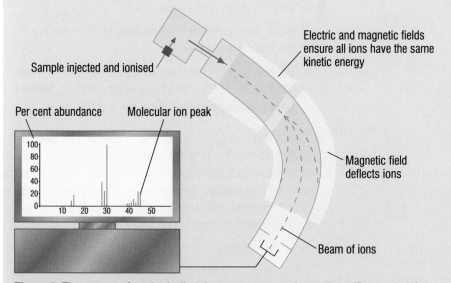

Figure 3 The pattern of peaks (called the mass spectrum) acts like a 'fingerprint' for unknown compounds. The pattern is quickly matched against a database of known compounds stored on computer.
NB You don't need to remember the details of how a mass spectrometer works.

Summary questions

1 Copy and complete using the words below:

   chromatography   database   mass   mixture   fingerprint

   Separating a .... of compounds can be carried out by gas ....
   Identifying compounds once they have been separated then uses
   techniques like .... spectrometry. The pattern of peaks is like a ....
   for each unknown compound. It is matched against known compounds
   on a computer ....

2 Describe how a mass spectrometer can be used to find the relative
   molecular mass of a compound.   [H]

Key points

● Compounds in a mixture can be separated using gas chromatography.

● Once separated, compounds can be identified using a mass spectrometer.

● The mass spectrometer can be used to find the relative molecular mass of a compound from its molecular ion peak.   [H]

Summary questions ⓚ

1 Match up the parts of the sentences:

a	Neutrons have a relative mass of …	A	… negligible mass compared to protons and neutrons.
b	Electrons have …	B	… 1 compared to protons.
c	Protons have a relative mass of …	C	… found in its nucleus.
d	Nearly all of an atom's mass is …	D	… 1 compared to neutrons.

2 Calculate the mass of 1 mole of each of the following compounds:

a H_2O

b CH_4

c MnO_2

d Al_2O_3

e K_2CO_3

f $KMnO_4$

g $Mn(OH)_2$

(A_r values: C = 12, O = 16, Al = 27, H = 1, Ca = 40, K = 39, Mn = 55)

3 How many moles of:

a Ag atoms are there in 108 g of silver,

b P atoms are there in 93 g of phosphorus,

c Ag atoms are there in 27 g of silver,

d P atoms are there in 6.2 g of phosphorus,

e Fe atoms are there in 0.56 g of iron,

f P_4 molecules are there in 6.2 g of phosphorus?

(A_r values: Ag = 108, P = 31, Fe = 56)

4 a The chemical formula of methane is CH_4. Use the relative atomic masses in question 2 to work out the percentage by mass of carbon in methane.

b In 32 g of methane, work out the mass of hydrogen present in the compound.

5 When aluminium reacts with bromine, 4.05 g of aluminium reacts with 36.0 g of bromine. What is the empirical formula of aluminium bromide?

(A_r values: Al = 27, Br = 80)   **[H]**

6 In a lime kiln, calcium carbonate is decomposed to calcium oxide:

$$CaCO_3 \rightarrow CaO + CO_2$$

50.0 tonnes of calcium carbonate gave 26.6 tonnes of calcium oxide. Calculate the percentage yield for the process.

(A_r values: Ca = 40, O = 16, C = 12)   **[H]**

7 a What is a reversible reaction?

b How does a reversible reaction differ from an 'ordinary' reaction?

c Ethene (C_2H_4) reacting with steam (H_2O) to form ethanol (C_2H_5OH) is a reversible reaction. Write the balanced symbol equation for this reaction.

8 Sulfur is mined in Poland and is brought to Britain in ships. The sulfur is used to make sulfuric acid. Sulfur is burned in air to produce sulfur dioxide. Sulfur dioxide and air are passed over a heated catalyst to produce sulfur trioxide. Water is added to sulfur trioxide to produce sulfuric acid. The reactions are:

$$S + O_2 \rightarrow SO_2$$
$$2SO_2 + O_2 \rightleftharpoons 2SO_3$$
$$SO_3 + H_2O \rightarrow H_2SO_4$$

Relative atomic masses: H = 1; O = 16; S = 32

a How many moles of sulfuric acid are produced from one mole of sulfur?

b Calculate the maximum mass of sulfuric acid that can be produced from 32 kg of sulfur.

c In an industrial process the mass of sulfuric acid that was produced from 32 kg of sulfur was 94.08 kg. Use your answer to part **b** to calculate the percentage yield of this process.

d Suggest two reasons why the yield of the industrial process was less than the maximum yield.

e Give two reasons why the industrial process should produce a yield that is as close to the maximum yield as possible.   **[H]**

AQA Examination-style questions k

1 a An atom of phosphorus can be represented as:

$$^{31}_{15}P$$

   i What is the number of protons in this atom of phosphorus? (1)

   ii What is the number of neutrons in this atom of phosphorus? (1)

   iii What are the number of electrons in this atom of phosphorus? (1)

b A different atom of phosphorus can be represented as:

$$^{32}_{15}P$$

   i What are these two atoms of phosphorus known as? (1)

   ii Give one way in which these two atoms of phosphorus are different. (1)

2 Toothpastes often contain fluoride ions to help protect teeth from attack by bacteria.

Some toothpastes contain tin(II) fluoride.

This compound has the formula SnF_2.

a Calculate the relative formula mass (M_r) of SnF_2.

(Relative atomic masses: F = 19; Sn = 119) (2)

b Calculate the percentage by mass of fluorine in SnF_2. (2)

c A tube of toothpaste contains 1.2 g of SnF_2. Calculate the mass of fluorine in this tube of toothpaste. (1)

AQA, 2008

3 The diagram shows what happens when ammonium chloride is heated.

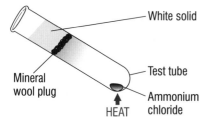

The reaction that takes place is:

$NH_4Cl(s) \rightleftharpoons NH_3(g) + HCl(g)$

a What does $\rightleftharpoons$ in the equation mean? (1)

b Explain why the white solid appears near the top of the test tube. (2)

4 The diagram shows the main parts of an instrumental method called gas chromatography linked to mass spectroscopy (GC–MS).

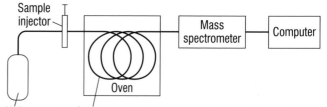

This method separates a mixture of compounds and then helps to identify each of the compounds in the mixture.

a In which part of the apparatus:

   i is the mixture separated? (1)

   ii is the relative molecular mass of each of the compounds in the mixture measured? (1)

   iii are the results of the experiment recorded? (1)

b **i** Athletes sometimes take drugs because the drugs improve their performance. One of these drugs is ephedrine.

Ephedrine has the formula:

$C_{10}H_{15}NO$

What relative molecular mass (M_r) would be recorded by GC–MS if ephedrine was present in a blood sample taken from an athlete?

Show clearly how you work out your answer.

(Relative atomic masses: H = 1; C = 12; N = 14; O = 16.) (2)

   ii Another drug is amphetamine, which has the formula: $C_9H_{13}N$

The relative molecular mass (M_r) of amphetamine is 135.

Calculate the percentage by mass of nitrogen in amphetamine. (Relative atomic mass: N = 14.) (2)

c Athletes are regularly tested for drugs at international athletics events. An instrumental method such as GC–MS is better than methods such as titration.

Suggest why. (2)

AQA, 2010

5 A chemist thought a liquid hydrocarbon was hexane, C_6H_{14}.

Relative atomic masses: H = 1; C = 12

a Calculate the percentage of carbon in hexane. (2)

b The chemist analysed the liquid hydrocarbon and found that it contained 85.7% carbon. Calculate the empirical formula of the hydrocarbon based on this result. You must show your working to gain full marks. (4)

c Was the liquid hydrocarbon hexane? Explain your answer. **[H]** (1)

C2 4.1 How fast?

Learning objectives

- What do we mean by the rate of a chemical reaction?
- How can we find out the rate of a chemical reaction?

Figure 1 All living things depend on very precise control of the many chemical reactions happening inside their cells

The rate of a chemical reaction tells us how fast reactants turn into products. In your body, there are lots of reactions taking place all the time. They happen at rates which supply your cells with what they need, whenever required.

Reaction rate is also very important in the chemical industry. Any industrial process has to make money by producing useful products. This means we must make the amount of product needed as cheaply as possible. If it takes too long to produce, it will be hard to make a profit when it is sold. The rate of the reaction must be fast enough to make it quickly and safely.

> a What do we mean by the *rate* of a chemical reaction?
> b Why is understanding the rate of reactions so important in industry?

How can we find out the rate of reactions?

Reactions happen at all sorts of different rates. Some are really fast, such as a firework exploding. Others are very slow, such as a piece of iron rusting.

There are two ways we can work out the rate of a chemical reaction. We can find out how quickly the reactants are used up as they make products. Or we can find out how quickly the products of the reaction are made.

Here are three ways we can make these kinds of measurement.

Practical

Measuring the decreasing mass of a reaction mixture

We can measure the rate at which the *mass* of a reaction mixture changes if the reaction gives off a gas. As the reaction takes place, the mass of the reaction mixture decreases. We can measure and record the mass at time intervals which we decide.

Some balances can be attached to a computer to monitor the loss in mass continuously.

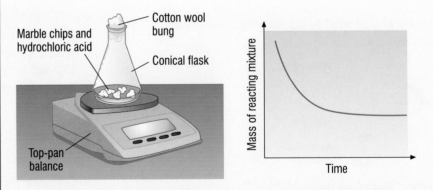

- Why is the cotton wool placed in the neck of the conical flask?
- How would the line on the graph differ if you plot 'Loss in mass' on the vertical axis?

Safety: Wear eye protection.

Practical

Measuring the increasing volume of gas given off

If a reaction produces a gas, we can use the gas to find out the rate of reaction. We do this by collecting the gas and measuring its volume at time intervals.

● What are the sources of error when measuring the volume of gas?

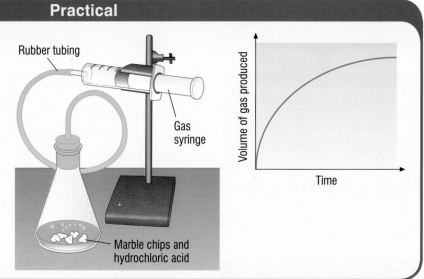

Rubber tubing

Gas syringe

Marble chips and hydrochloric acid

Volume of gas produced

Time

Practical

Measuring the decreasing light passing through a solution

Some reactions in solution make an insoluble solid (precipitate). This makes the solution go cloudy. We can use this to measure the rate at which the solid appears.

The reaction is set up in a flask. Under the flask, we put on a piece of paper marked with a cross. Then we can record the time taken for the cross to disappear. The shorter the time, the faster the reaction rate.

Or we can use a light sensor and data logger. Then we measure the amount of light that passes through the solution, as the graph shows.

● What are the advantages of using a light sensor rather than the 'disappearing cross' method?

Light transmitted

Time

We can summarise these methods of working out the rate of a reaction using this equation:

Rate of reaction = $\dfrac{\text{amount of reactant used or amount of product formed}}{\text{time}}$

Summary questions

1 Copy and complete using the words below:

products   rate   time   reactants   slope

Measuring the amount of .... which are used up over time or the amount of .... made over time are two ways of finding out the .... of a reaction. The .... of the lines on graphs drawn from these experiments tells us about the rate at any given ....

2 Sketch graphs to show the results of:
   a i   measuring the mass of products formed in a reaction over time.
     ii   measuring the mass of reactants used up in a reaction over time.
   b What does the slope of the graphs at any particular time in part **a** tell us about the reaction?

Key points

● We can find out the rate of a chemical reaction by following the amount of reactants used up over time.

● Alternatively, we can find out the rate of reaction by following the amount of products made over time.

● The slope of the line at any given time on the graphs drawn from such experiments tells us the rate of reaction at that time. The steeper the slope, the faster the reaction.

C2 4.2

Collision theory and surface area

Learning objectives

- What affects the rate of a chemical reaction?

- What is collision theory?

- How does collision theory explain the effect of surface area on reaction rate?

Figure 1 There is no doubt that the chemicals in these fireworks have reacted. But how can we explain what happens in a chemical reaction?

Figure 2 Cooking – an excellent example of controlling reaction rates!

In everyday life we control the rates of chemical reactions. People often do it without knowing! For example, cooking cakes in an oven or revving up a car engine. In chemistry we need to know what affects the rate of reactions. We also need to explain why each factor affects the rate of a reaction.

There are four main factors which affect the rate of chemical reactions:

- temperature
- surface area
- concentration of solutions or pressure of gases
- presence of a catalyst.

Reactions can only take place when the particles (atoms, ions or molecules) of reactants come together. But the reacting particles don't just have to bump into each other. They also need enough energy to react when they collide. This is known as **collision theory**.

The smallest amount of energy that particles must have before they can react is called the **activation energy**.

So reactions are more likely to happen between reactant particles if we:

- increase the chance of reacting particles colliding with each other
- increase the energy that they have when they collide.

If we increase the chance of particles reacting, we will also increase the rate of reaction.

> **a** What must happen before two particles have a chance of reacting?
> **b** Particles must have a minimum amount of energy to be able to react. What is this energy called?

Surface area and reaction rate **k**

Imagine lighting a campfire. You don't pile large logs together and try to set them alight. You use small pieces of wood to begin with. Doing this increases the surface area of the wood. This means there is more wood exposed to react with oxygen in the air.

When a solid reacts in a solution, the size of the pieces of solid affects the rate of the reaction. The particles inside a large lump of solid are not in contact with the solution, so they can't react. The particles inside the solid have to wait for the particles on the surface to react first.

In smaller lumps, or in a powder, each tiny piece of solid is surrounded by solution. More particles are exposed to attack. This means that reactions can take place much more quickly.

> **c** Which has the larger surface area – a log or the same mass of small pieces of wood?
> **d** How does the surface area of a solid affect its rate of reaction?

Practical

Which burns faster?

Make sure you have a heatproof mat under the Bunsen burner and you must wear eye protection.

Try igniting a 2 cm length of magnesium ribbon and time how long it takes to burn.

Take a small spatula tip of magnesium powder and sprinkle it into the Bunsen flame.

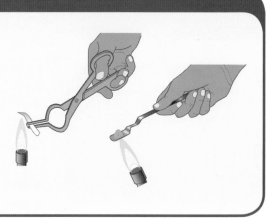

- What safety precautions should you take in this experiment?
- Explain your observations.

Practical

Investigating the effect of surface area

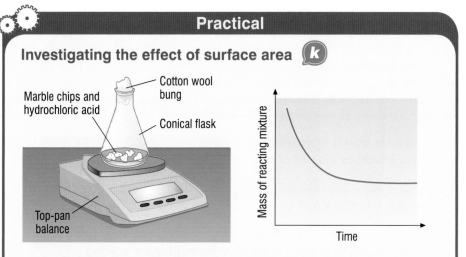

Marble chips and hydrochloric acid — Cotton wool bung — Conical flask — Top-pan balance

Mass of reacting mixture / Time

In this investigation you will be measuring the mass against time for different sizes of marble (calcium carbonate) chips. You need at least two different sizes of marble chips in order to vary the surface area.

- What variables should you control to make this a fair test?
- Why does this method of finding out the rate of reaction work?
- Use the data collected to draw a graph. Explain what the graph shows. (A data logger would help to plot a graph of the results.)

Safety: Wear eye protection.

Summary questions

1 Copy and complete using the words below:

energy   activation   collide   frequently   minimum

Particles can react with each other only when they .... with sufficient .... Reaction rates increase when collisions are more energetic and/or happen more .... The .... amount of energy needed for particles to react is known as the .... energy.

2 Draw a diagram to explain why it is easier to light a fire using small pieces of wood rather than large logs.

3 Why do you digest your food more quickly if you chew it well before you swallow it?

Key points

- Particles must collide, with a certain amount of energy, before they can react.

- The minimum amount of energy that particles must have in order to react is called the activation energy.

- The rate of a chemical reaction increases if the surface area of any solid reactants is increased. This increases the frequency of collisions between reacting particles.

C2 4.3 The effect of temperature

Learning objectives

● How does increasing the temperature affect the rate of reactions?

● How does collision theory explain this effect?

Figure 1 Lowering the temperature will slow down the reactions that make foods go off

Figure 2 Moving faster means it's more likely that you'll bump into someone else – and the collision will be harder too!

When we increase the temperature, it always increases the rate of reaction. We can use fridges and freezers to reduce the temperature and slow down the rate of reactions. When food goes off it is because of chemical reactions. Reducing the temperature slows down these reactions.

Collision theory tells us why raising the temperature increases the rate of a reaction. There are two reasons:

● particles collide more often

● particles collide with more energy.

Particles collide more often

When we heat up a substance, energy is transferred to its particles. In solutions and in gases, this means that the particles move around faster. And when particles move faster they collide more often. Imagine a lot of people walking around in the school playground blindfolded. They may bump into each other occasionally. However, if they start running around, they will bump into each other much more often.

When particles collide more frequently, there are more chances for them to react. This increases the rate of reaction.

Particles collide with more energy

Particles that are moving around more quickly have more energy. This means that any collisions they have are much more energetic. It's like two people colliding when they're running rather than when they are walking.

When we increase the temperature of a reacting mixture, a higher proportion of the collisions will result in a reaction taking place. This is because a higher proportion of particles have energy greater than the activation energy. This second factor has a greater effect on rate than the increased frequency of collisions.

Around room temperature, if we increase the temperature of a reaction by 10°C the rate of the reaction will roughly double.

a Why does increasing the temperature increase the rate of a reaction?

b How much does a 10°C rise in temperature increase reaction rate at room temperature?

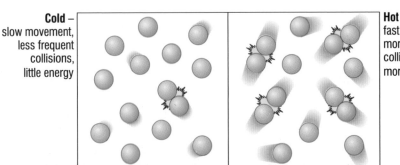

Figure 3 More frequent collisions, with more energy – both of these factors increase the rate of a chemical reaction caused by increasing the temperature

Practical

The effect of temperature on rate of reaction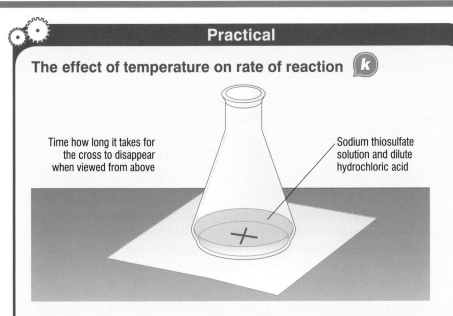

Time how long it takes for the cross to disappear when viewed from above

Sodium thiosulfate solution and dilute hydrochloric acid

When we react sodium thiosulfate solution and hydrochloric acid it makes sulfur. The sulfur is insoluble in water. This makes the solution go cloudy. We can record the length of time it takes for the solution to go cloudy at different temperatures.

● Which variables do you have to control to make this a fair test?
● Why is it difficult to get accurate timings by eye in this investigation?
● How can you improve the **precision** of the data you collect?

Safety: Wear eye protection. Take care if you are an asthmatic.

The results of an investigation like this can be plotted on a graph (see opposite).

The graph shows how the time for the solution to go cloudy changes with temperature.

c What happens to the time it takes the solution to go cloudy as the temperature increases?

Maths skills

As one goes up, the other comes down

In the experiment opposite we can measure the time for an X to disappear as a precipitate forms. This means that the longer the time, the slower the rate of reaction. There is an inverse relationship between time and rate. So as time increases, rate decreases. We say the rate is proportional to 1/time (also written as time^{-1}). Therefore, we can plot a graph of temperature against 1/time to investigate the effect of temperature on rate of reaction.   **[H]**

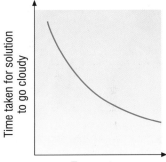

Summary questions

1 Copy and complete using the words below:

chemical   collide   decreases   doubles   energy   off   quickly   rate   reducing   rise

When we increase the temperature of a reacting mixture, we increase its .... of reaction. The higher temperature makes the particles move more .... so they .... more often and the collisions have more .... At room temperature, a temperature .... of about 10 °C roughly .... the reaction rate. This explains why we use fridges and freezers. .... the temperature .... the rate of the .... reactions which make food go ....

2 Water in a pressure cooker boils at a much higher temperature than water in a saucepan because it is under pressure. Why does food take longer to cook in a pan than it does in a pressure cooker?

Key points

● Reactions happen more quickly as the temperature increases.

● Increasing the temperature increases the rate of reaction because particles collide more frequently and more energetically. More of the collisions result in a reaction because a higher proportion of particles have energy greater than the activation energy.

C2 4.4

The effect of concentration or pressure ⓚ

Learning objectives

- How does increasing the concentration of reactants in solutions affect the rate of reaction?

- How does increasing the pressure of reacting gases affect the rate of reaction?

Some of our most beautiful buildings are made of limestone or marble. These buildings have stood for centuries. However, they are now crumbling away at a greater rate than before. This is because both limestone and marble are mainly calcium carbonate. This reacts with acids, leaving the stone soft and crumbly. The rate of this reaction has speeded up because the concentration of acids in rainwater has been steadily increasing.

Increasing the concentration of reactants in a solution increases the rate of reaction. That's because there are more particles of the reactants moving around in the same volume of solution. The more 'crowded' together the reactant particles are, the more likely it is that they will collide. So the more frequent collisions result in a faster reaction.

Increasing the pressure of reacting gases has the same effect. It squashes the gas particles more closely together. We have more particles of gas in a given space. This increases the chance that they will collide and react. So increasing the pressure speeds up the rate of the reaction.

a Why does increasing concentration or pressure increase reaction rate?

Figure 1 Limestone statues are damaged by acid rain. This damage happens more quickly as the concentration of the acids in rainwater increases.

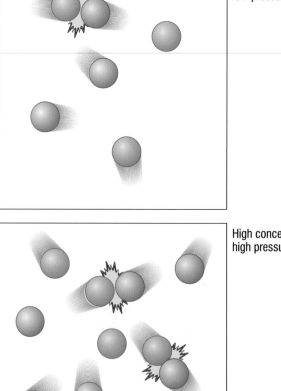

Low concentration/ low pressure

High concentration/ high pressure

Figure 2 Increasing concentration and pressure both mean that particles are closer together. This increases the frequency of collisions between particles, so the reaction rate increases.

Practical

Investigating the effect of concentration on rate of reaction

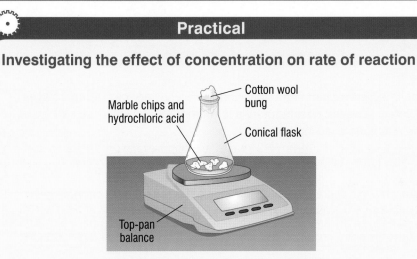

Cotton wool bung
Marble chips and hydrochloric acid
Conical flask
Top-pan balance

We can investigate the effect of changing concentration by reacting marble chips with different concentrations of hydrochloric acid:

$$CaCO_3 + 2HCl \rightarrow CaCl_2 + CO_2 + H_2O$$

We can find the rate of reaction by plotting the mass of the reaction mixture over time. The mass will decrease as carbon dioxide gas is given off in the reaction.

● How do you make this a fair test?

● What conclusion can you draw from your results?

Safety: Wear eye protection.

AQA **Examiner's tip**

Increasing concentration or pressure does not increase the energy with which the particles collide. However, it does increase the frequency of collisions.

If we plot the results of an investigation like the one above on a graph they look like the graph opposite:

The graph shows how the mass of the reaction mixture decreases over time at three different concentrations.

b Which line on the graph shows the fastest reaction? How can you tell?

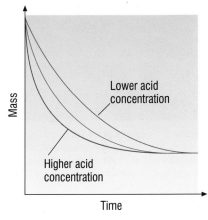

Mass
Lower acid concentration
Higher acid concentration
Time

Summary questions

1 Copy and complete using the words below:

collisions concentration faster frequency number pressure rate volume

The .... of a reaction is affected by the .... of reactants in solutions and by the .... if the reactants are gases. Both of these tell us the .... of particles that there are in a certain .... of the reaction mixture. Increasing these will increase the .... of .... between reacting particles, making .... reactions.

2 Acidic cleaners are designed to remove limescale when they are used neat. They do not work as well when they are diluted. Using your knowledge of collision theory, explain why this is.

3 You could also follow the reaction in the Practical box above by measuring the volume of gas given off over time. Sketch a graph of volume of gas against time for three different concentrations. Label the three lines as high, medium and low concentration.

Key points

● Increasing the concentration of reactants in solutions increases the frequency of collisions between particles, and so increases the rate of reaction.

● Increasing the pressure of reacting gases also increases the frequency of collisions and so increases the rate of reaction.

C2 4.5

The effect of catalysts ⓚ

Learning objectives

- What is a catalyst?
- How do catalysts affect the rate of reactions?

Figure 1 Catalysts are all around us, in the natural world and in industry. The catalysts in living things are called enzymes. Our planet would be very different without catalysts.

Sometimes a reaction might only work if we use very high temperatures or pressures. This can cost industry a lot of money. However, we can speed up some reactions by using **catalysts**.

a Apart from using a catalyst, how can we speed up a reaction?

A catalyst is a substance which increases the rate of a reaction. However, it is not changed chemically itself at the end of the reaction.

A catalyst is not used up in the reaction. So it can be used over and over again.

We need different catalysts for different reactions. Many of the catalysts we use in industry involve transition metals. For example, iron is used to make ammonia. Platinum is used to make nitric acid.

b How is a catalyst affected by a chemical reaction?

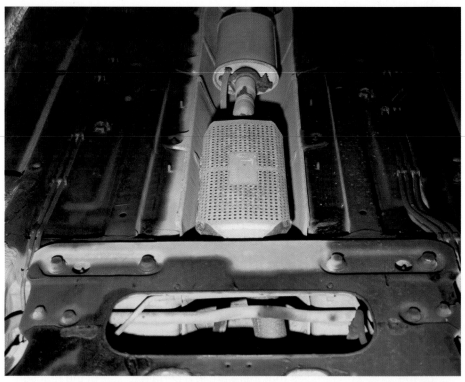

Figure 2 The transition metals platinum and palladium are used in the catalytic converters in cars

We normally use catalysts in the form of powders, pellets or fine gauzes. This gives them the biggest possible surface area.

c Why is a catalyst in the form of pellets more effective than a whole lump of the catalyst?

Not only does a catalyst speed up a reaction, but it does not get used up in the reaction. We can use a tiny amount of catalyst to speed up a reaction over and over again.

Practical

Investigating catalysis 🄚

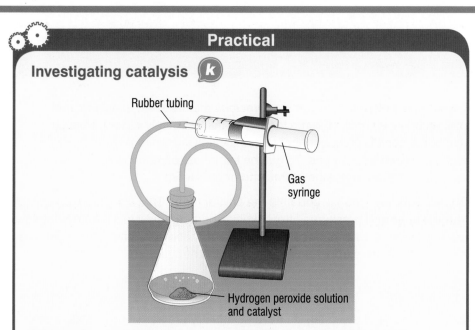

Rubber tubing

Gas syringe

Hydrogen peroxide solution and catalyst

Figure 3 This catalyst is used in the form of pellets to give the largest possible surface area.

We can investigate the effect of different catalysts on the rate of a reaction. We will look at hydrogen peroxide solution decomposing:

$$2H_2O_2 \rightarrow 2H_2O + O_2$$

The reaction produces oxygen gas. We can collect this in a gas syringe using the apparatus shown above.

We can investigate the effect of many different substances on the rate of this reaction. Examples include manganese(IV) oxide and potassium iodide.

● State the independent variable in this investigation.

A table of the time taken to produce a certain volume of oxygen can then tell us which catalyst makes the reaction go fastest.

● What type of graph would you use to show the results of your investigation? Why?

Safety: Wear eye protection.

AQA Examiner's tip

Catalysts change only the rate of reactions. They do not change the products.

Summary questions

1 Copy and complete using the words below:

remains   increases   reaction   used

A catalyst _____ the rate of a chemical reaction. However, it is not _____ up and _____ the same chemically after the _____ .

2 Solid catalysts used in chemical processes are often shaped as tiny beads or cylinders with holes through them. Why are they made in these shapes?

3 Why is the number of moles of catalyst needed to speed up a chemical reaction very small compared with the number of moles of reactants?

Key points

● A catalyst speeds up the rate of a chemical reaction.

● A catalyst is not used up during a chemical reaction.

● Different catalysts are needed for different reactions.

C2 4.6 Catalysts in action

Learning objectives

- Why are catalysts used in so many industrial processes?

- How are new catalysts developed and why are there so many different catalysts?

- What are the disadvantages of using catalysts in industry?

Catalysts are often very expensive precious metals. Gold, platinum and palladium are all costly but are the most effective catalysts for particular reactions. But it is often cheaper to use a catalyst than to pay for the extra energy needed without one. To get the same rate of reaction without a catalyst would require higher temperatures and/or pressures.

So catalysts save money and help the environment. That's because using high temperatures and pressures often involves burning fossil fuels. So operating at lower temperatures and pressures conserves these non-renewable resources. It also stops more carbon dioxide entering the atmosphere.

> **a** Why do catalysts save a chemical company money?

However, many of the catalysts used in industry are transition metals or their compounds. These are often toxic. If they escape into the environment, they build up inside living things. Eventually they poison them. For example, the platinum and palladium used in catalytic converters slowly escape from car exhausts.

So chemists are working to develop new catalysts that are harmless to the environment. The search for the ideal catalyst is often a bit like trial and error. Each reaction is unique. Once a catalyst is found it might be improved by adding small amounts of other chemicals to it. All this takes a lot of time to investigate. However, the research is guided by knowledge of similar catalysed reactions. This knowledge is growing all the time.

Figure 1 Chinese scientists have recently developed a new catalyst for making biodiesel from vegetable oils. It's made from shrimp shells, and is cheaper and more efficient than conventional catalysts. The process that uses the new catalyst also causes less pollution.

Future development

Chemists have developed new techniques to look at reactions. They can now follow the reactions that happen on the surface of the metals in a catalytic converter. These are very fast reactions lasting only a fraction of a second. Knowing how the reactions take place will help them to design new catalysts.

Nanoparticles are also at the cutting edge of work on new catalysts. Scientists can arrange atoms into the best shapes for catalysing a particular reaction they have studied. A small mass of these catalysts has a huge surface area. This has raised hopes that fuel cells will one day take over from petrol and diesel to run cars.

Catalysts in medicine

The catalysts used in making new drugs also contain precious metal compounds. The metal is bonded to an organic molecule. But now chemists can make these catalysts without the metal. The metal was needed to make a stable compound. However, research has resulted in a breakthrough which will mean much cheaper catalysts. There is also no risk of contaminating the drug made with a toxic transition metal.

b Why could it be unsafe to use compounds of transition metals to catalyse reactions to make drugs?

Enzymes

Enzymes are the very efficient catalysts found in living things. For years we've been using enzymes to help clean our clothes. Biological washing powders contain enzymes that help to 'break apart' stain molecules such as proteins at low temperatures. The low temperature washes save energy.

Low-temperature enzyme reactions are the basis of the biotechnology industry. Enzymes are soluble so would have to be separated from the products they make. However, scientists can bind them to a solid. The solution of reactants flows over the solid. No time or money has to be wasted separating out the enzymes to use again. The process can run continuously.

⊂⊃ **links**

For information about nanoparticles, look back to C2 2.6 Nanoscience.

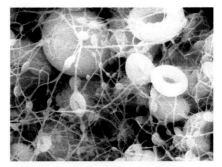

Figure 2 Scientists are developing long nanowires of platinum to use as catalysts in fuel cells. This photo is from an electron microscope. The wires are 1/50000th of the width of a human hair. The breakthrough has been made in making them over a centimetre in length.

Key points

● Catalysts are used whenever possible in industry to increase rate of reaction and reduce energy costs.

● Traditional catalysts are often transition metals or their compounds, which can be toxic and harm the environment if they escape.

● Modern catalysts are being developed in industry which result in less waste and are safer for the environment.

Summary questions

1 Give two ways in which catalysts are beneficial to the chemical industry.

2 What are the disadvantages of using transition metals or their compounds as catalysts?

3 Do some research to find out four industrial processes that make products using catalysts. Write a word equation for each reaction and name the catalyst used.

C2 4.9

Using energy transfers from reactions

Learning objectives

- How can we use the energy from exothermic reactions?

- How can we use the cooling effect of endothermic reactions?

- What are the advantages and disadvantages of using exothermic and endothermic reactions in the uses described?

Demonstration

Crystallisation of a supersaturated solution

Dissolve 700 g of sodium ethanoate in 50 cm³ of hot water in a conical flask. Then let the solution cool to room temperature. Now add a small crystal of sodium ethanoate.

- What do you see happen? What does the outside of the flask feel like?

Figure 1 Here is a hand warmer based on the recrystallisation of sodium ethanoate

Warming up

Chemical hand and body warmers can be very useful. These products use exothermic reactions to warm you up. People can take hand warmers to places they know will get very cold. For example, spectators at outdoor sporting events in winter can warm their hands up. People usually use the body warmers to help ease aches and pains.

Some hand warmers can only be used once. An example of this type uses the oxidation of iron to release energy. Iron turns into hydrated iron(III) oxide in an exothermic reaction. The reaction is similar to rusting. Sodium chloride (common salt) is used as a catalyst. This type of hand warmer is disposable. It can be used only once but it lasts for hours.

Other hand warmers can be reused many times. These are based on the formation of crystals from solutions of a salt. The salt used is often sodium ethanoate. A supersaturated solution is prepared. We do this by dissolving as much of the salt as possible in hot water. The solution is then allowed to cool.

A small metal disc in the plastic pack is used to start the exothermic change. When you press this a few times small particles of metal are scraped off. These 'seed' (or start off) the crystallisation. The crystals spread throughout the solution, giving off energy. They work for about 30 minutes.

To reuse the warmer, you simply put the solid pack into boiling water to re-dissolve the crystals. When cool, the pack is ready to activate again.

a Common salt is used as a *catalyst* in some disposable hand warmers. What does this mean?

Exothermic reactions are also used in self-heating cans (see Figure 2). The reaction used to release the energy is usually:

$$\text{calcium oxide} + \text{water} \rightarrow \text{calcium hydroxide}$$

You press a button in the base of the can. This breaks a seal and lets the water and calcium oxide mix. Coffee is available in these self-heating cans.

Development took years and cost millions of pounds. Even then, over a third of the can was taken up with the reactants to release energy. Also, in some early versions, the temperature of the coffee did not rise high enough in cold conditions.

b Which solid is usually used in the base of self-heating coffee cans?

Activity

Hot food

Mountaineers and explorers can take 'self-heating' foods with them on their journeys. One uses the energy released when calcium oxide reacts with water to heat the food.

Design a self-heating, disposable food container for stew.

- Draw a labelled diagram of your container and explain how it works.

- What are the safety issues involved in using your product?

Cooling down

Endothermic processes can be used to cool things down. For example, chemical cold packs usually contain ammonium nitrate and water. When ammonium nitrate dissolves it takes in energy from its surroundings, making them colder. These cold packs are used as emergency treatment for sports injuries. The coldness reduces swelling and numbs pain.

The ammonium nitrate and water (sometimes as a gel) are kept separate in the pack. When squeezed or struck the bag inside the water pack breaks releasing ammonium nitrate. The instant cold packs work for about 20 minutes.

They can only be used once but are ideal where there is no ice available to treat a knock or strain.

The same endothermic change can also be used to chill cans of drinks.

TO HEAT CONTAINER
Turn container UPSIDE DOWN before opening and follow instructions.

STEP 4
HOT SPOT turns from pink to white when beverage is hot. (6–8 minutes)

STEP 5
Once hot, shake 5 to 10 seconds then twist lid to align opening with pull-tab. Open and enjoy.

TWIST WHEN HOT

STEP 3
Wait 5 SECONDS and turn can right side up
coloured water drains into the activation chamber.

STEP 2
Place container on flat surface. Using thumb, FIRMLY push button DOWNWARD until internal foil seal tears and

STEP 1
PULL off tamper-proof metal bottom

Figure 2 Development of this self-heating can in the USA took about 10 years. The pink circle on the can turns white when the coffee is hot enough. This takes 6–8 minutes.

Figure 3 Instant cold packs can be applied as soon as an injury occurs to minimise damage to the sportsperson

Summary questions

1 a Describe how a disposable hand warmer works.
 b Describe how a re-usable hand warmer works.
 c Give an advantage and a disadvantage of each type of hand warmer.
 d Name one use of an exothermic reaction in the food industry.

2 a Give two uses of endothermic changes.
 b Which endothermic change is often used in cold packs?

C2 5.7 Electrolysis of brine

Practical

Electrolysing brine in the lab

Turn off the electricity once the tubes are nearly full of gas to avoid inhaling chlorine gas (toxic).

- How can you positively test for the gases collected?

Test the solution near the negative electrode with universal indicator solution.

- What does the indicator tell us?

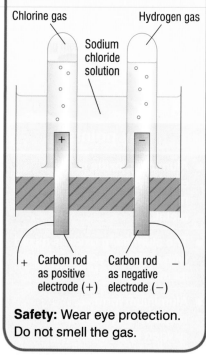

Chlorine gas   Hydrogen gas

Sodium chloride solution

+ Carbon rod as positive electrode (+)   Carbon rod as negative electrode (−) −

Safety: Wear eye protection. Do not smell the gas.

∞ links

For information about what happens when two ions are attracted to an electrode, see C2 5.5 Changes at the electrodes.

The electrolysis of **brine** (concentrated sodium chloride solution) is a very important industrial process. When we pass an electric current through brine we get three products:

- chlorine gas is produced at the positive electrode
- hydrogen gas is produced at the negative electrode
- sodium hydroxide solution is also formed.

We can summarise the electrolysis of brine as:

$$\text{sodium chloride solution} \xrightarrow{\text{electrolysis}} \text{hydrogen} + \text{chlorine} + \text{sodium hydroxide solution}$$

> **a** What are the three products made when we electrolyse brine?

At the positive electrode (+):

The negative chloride ions (Cl^-) are attracted to the positive electrode. When they get there, they each lose one electron. The chloride ions are oxidised, as they lose electrons. The chlorine atoms bond together in pairs and are given off as chlorine gas (Cl_2).

At the negative electrode (−):

There are H^+ ions in brine, formed when water breaks down:

$$H_2O \rightleftharpoons H^+ + OH^-$$

These positive hydrogen ions are attracted to the negative electrode. The sodium ions (Na^+) are also attracted to the same electrode. But remember in C2 5.5, we saw what happens when two ions are attracted to an electrode. It is the less reactive element that gets discharged. In this case, hydrogen ions are discharged and sodium ions stay in solution.

When the H^+ ions get to the negative electrode, they each gain one electron. The hydrogen ions are reduced, as they each gain an electron. The hydrogen atoms formed bond together in pairs and are given off as hydrogen gas (H_2).

The remaining solution:

You can test the solution around the negative electrode with indicator. It shows that the solution is alkaline. This is because we can think of brine as containing aqueous ions of Na^+ and Cl^- (from salt) and H^+ and OH^- (from water). The Cl^- and H^+ ions are removed during electrolysis. So this leaves a solution containing Na^+ and OH^- ions, i.e. a solution of sodium hydroxide.

Look at the way we can electrolyse brine in industry in Figure 1.

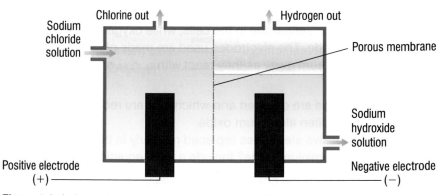

Chlorine out   Hydrogen out
Sodium chloride solution
Porous membrane
Sodium hydroxide solution
Positive electrode (+)   Negative electrode (−)

Figure 1 In industry, brine can be electrolysed in a cell in which the two electrodes are separated by a porous membrane. This is called a diaphragm cell.

Higher

Half equations for the electrolysis of brine

The half equations for what happens in the electrolysis of brine are:

At the positive electrode (+):

$$2Cl^-(aq) \rightarrow Cl_2(g) + 2e^-$$

[remember that this can also be written as: $2Cl^-(aq) - 2e^- \rightarrow Cl_2(g)$]

At the negative electrode (−):

$$2H^+(aq) + 2e^- \rightarrow H_2(g)$$

Using chlorine

We can react chlorine with the sodium hydroxide produced in the electrolysis of brine. This makes a solution of **bleach**. Bleach is very good at killing bacteria.

Chlorine is also important in making many other disinfectants, as well as plastics such as PVC.

b What is chlorine used for?

Using hydrogen

The hydrogen that we make by electrolysing brine is particularly pure. This makes it very useful in the food industry. We make margarine by reacting hydrogen with vegetable oils.

c What is hydrogen used for?

Using sodium hydroxide

The sodium hydroxide from the electrolysis of brine is used to make soap and paper. It is also used to make bleach (see above).

d What is sodium hydroxide used for?

Figure 2 The chlorine made when we electrolyse brine is used to kill bacteria in drinking water, and also in swimming pools

Summary questions

1 Copy and complete using the words below:

hydrogen   bleach   hydroxide   chlorine

When we pass an electric current through brine we can collect .... gas at the positive electrode, and .... gas at the negative electrode. Sodium .... solution is formed in the cell. Two of these products are also used to make ....

2 We can electrolyse *molten* sodium chloride. Compare the products formed with those from the electrolysis of sodium chloride solution. What are the differences?

3 For the electrolysis of brine, write half equations, including state symbols, for the reactions **a** at the positive electrode and **b** at the negative electrode. [H]

Key points

- When we electrolyse brine we get three products – chlorine gas, hydrogen gas and sodium hydroxide solution (an alkali).
- Chlorine is used to make bleach, which kills bacteria, and to make plastics.
- Hydrogen is used to make margarine.
- Sodium hydroxide is used to make bleach, paper and soap.

C3 1.5

Group 7 – the halogens ⓚ

Learning objectives

- How do the Group 7 elements behave?

- How do the properties of the Group 7 elements change going down the group?

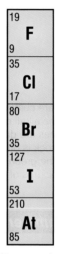

Figure 1 The Group 7 elements

Properties of the halogens

The Group 7 elements are called the halogens. They are a group of poisonous non-metals that have coloured vapours. They have fairly typical properties of non-metals.

- They have low melting points and boiling points.
- They are also poor conductors of energy and electricity.

As elements, the halogens all exist as molecules made up of pairs of atoms. The atoms are joined to each other by covalent bonds.

	F—F (F_2)	Cl—Cl (Cl_2)	Br—Br (Br_2)	I—I (I_2)
Melting Point (°C)	−220	−101	−7	114
Boiling Point (°C)	−188	−35	59	184

Figure 2 The halogens all form molecules made up of a pair of atoms, joined by a covalent bond. We call this type of molecule a diatomic molecule.

a What patterns can you spot in the properties of the halogens going down Group 7?

Reactions of the halogens

The electronic structure of the halogens determines the way they react with other elements. They all have seven electrons in their outermost shell (highest energy level). So they need to gain just one more electron to achieve the stable electronic structure of a noble gas. This means that the halogens take part in both ionic and covalent bonding.

	How the halogens react with hydrogen
$F_2(g) + H_2(g) \rightarrow 2HF(g)$	Explosive even at −200°C and in the dark
$Cl_2(g) + H_2(g) \rightarrow 2HCl(g)$	Explosive in sunlight / slow in the dark
$Br_2(g) + H_2(g) \rightarrow 2HBr(g)$	300°C + platinum catalyst
$I_2(g) + H_2(g) \rightleftharpoons 2HI(g)$	300°C + platinum catalyst (very slow, reversible)

b Look at the reactions of the halogens in the table above. What is the pattern in reactivity of the halogens going down Group 7?

The halogens all react with metals. They gain a single electron to give them a stable arrangement of electrons. They form ions with a 1− charge, e.g. F^-, Cl^-, Br^-. Examples of their ionic compounds include sodium chloride, NaCl, and iron(III) bromide, $FeBr_3$.

AQA *Examiner's tip*

In Group 7, reactivity *decreases* as you go down the group. However, in Group 1 reactivity *increases* going down the group.

Look at the dot and cross diagram of calcium chloride, CaCl₂, below:

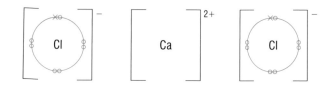

c Write down the formula of an iodide ion.

When a halogen reacts with another non-metal, the atoms of the halogen share electrons with the atoms of the other element. This gives the atoms of both elements a stable electronic structure. Therefore the compounds of halogens with non-metals contain covalent bonds.

Look at the dot and cross diagram of hydrogen chloride, HCl, below:

(Note that the circles need not be shown in dot and cross diagrams.)

Displacement reactions between halogens

We can use a more reactive halogen to displace a less reactive halogen from solutions of its salts.

Bromine displaces iodine from solution because it is more reactive than iodine. Chlorine will displace both iodine and bromine.

For example, chlorine will displace bromine:

chlorine + potassium bromide → potassium chloride + bromine

$$Cl_2(aq) + 2KBr(aq) \rightarrow 2KCl(aq) + Br_2(aq)$$

Obviously fluorine, the most reactive of the halogens, would displace all of the others. However, it reacts so strongly with water that we cannot carry out any reactions in aqueous solutions.

Summary questions

1 Copy and complete using the words below:

covalent halogens ionic less most top

Group 7 elements are also called the .... Fluorine, at the .... of the group, is the .... reactive, while iodine is much .... reactive. They react with other non-metals to form compounds which have .... bonds. With metals they react to form .... compounds.

2 **a** Write a word equation for the reaction of sodium with bromine.
   b Write a word equation for the reaction of bromine water with potassium iodide solution.

3 Write a balanced symbol equation, including state symbols, for the reaction of:
   a potassium metal with iodine vapour   [H]
   b chlorine water with sodium iodide solution.   [H]

Practical

Displacement reactions

Add bromine water to potassium iodide solution in a test tube. Then try some other combinations of solutions of halogens and potassium halides.

● Record your results in a table.
● Explain your observations.

Key points

● The halogens all form ions with a single negative charge in their ionic compounds with metals.

● The halogens form covalent compounds by sharing electrons with other non-metals.

● A more reactive halogen can displace a less reactive halogen from a solution of one of its salts.

● The reactivity of the halogens decreases going down the group.

C3 3.2

Energy transfers in solutions (k)

Learning objectives

- How can we measure the energy change for a reaction that takes place in solution?

links

For more information about using simple calorimeters, look back at C2 4.7 Exothermic and endothermic reactions.

We have used a simple calorimeter to measure temperature changes. We used a polystyrene cup and a thermometer to monitor reactions in solution.

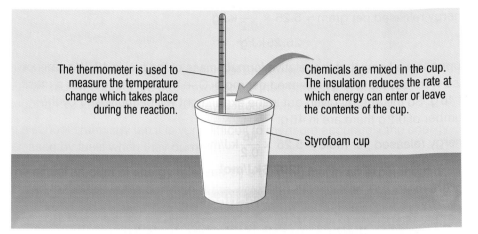

The thermometer is used to measure the temperature change which takes place during the reaction.

Chemicals are mixed in the cup. The insulation reduces the rate at which energy can enter or leave the contents of the cup.

Styrofoam cup

Figure 1 A simple calorimeter used to measure energy changes in solution. The polystyrene is a good thermal insulator so helps to minimise energy transfer through the sides of the container during reactions. A lid on the calorimeter reduces energy transfer to the surroundings even further.

However, we have now seen how we can calculate actual energy changes using:

$$Q = mc\Delta T$$

In words:

energy released = mass of water heated × specific heat capacity of water × rise in temperature

a Why is polystyrene a good material to use for a calorimeter for reactions in solution?

In these calculations we will assume that the solutions behave like water. So $1\,cm^3$ of solution has a mass of $1\,g$. Also solutions have a specific heat capacity of $4.2\,J/g\,°C$. Therefore $4.2\,J$ of energy raise the temperature of $1\,g$ of solution by $1\,°C$. Look at the worked example opposite.

AQA Examiner's tip

You do not have to learn the equation $Q = mc\Delta T$

In the exam this equation will be provided for you but you should know how to use it.

Practical

Measuring energy changes in reactions

We can use a simple polystyrene calorimeter to work out the energy changes in the following:

- iron filings + copper sulfate solution (a displacement reaction)
- magnesium ribbon + hydrochloric acid
- sodium hydroxide + hydrochloric acid (a neutralisation reaction)
- dissolving potassium nitrate, anhydrous copper sulfate, and other salts.

Maths skills

Worked example

A simple calorimeter is used to measure the energy change in the reaction:

$$A + B \rightarrow C$$

60 cm³ of a solution containing 0.1 moles of A is mixed with 40 cm³ of a solution containing 0.1 moles of B. The temperature of the two solutions before mixing is 19.6 °C. After mixing them, the maximum temperature reached is 26.1 °C.

Step 1 – calculate the temperature change:

temperature change = 26.1 °C – 19.6 °C
$$= 6.5 °C$$

Step 2 – calculate the energy change:

$$Q = mc\Delta T$$

The mass of solution heated up in the reaction is 60 g + 40 g = 100 g

energy change = 100 g × 4.2 J/g°C × 6.5 °C
$$= 2730 J$$
$$= 2.73 kJ$$

This is the energy change when 0.1 moles of reactants A and B are mixed. So when 1 mole of reactants are mixed there will be ten times as much energy released (1 mole is 10 × 0.1 moles)

$$= 2.73 kJ \times 10$$

$$= 27.3 kJ$$

So this experiment gives the energy change for the reaction:

$$A + B \rightarrow C$$

as **27.3 kJ/mol**. (The temperature rises so the reaction is exothermic).

b Which has the higher energy content in A + B → C, the reactants or the product?

links

For more information on energy level diagrams, see C3 3.3 Energy level diagrams.

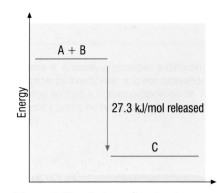

Figure 2 Here is the energy level diagram for the reaction A + B → C

Summary questions

1 Copy and complete using the words below:

energy   polystyrene   temperature   calorimeter

A .... cup can be used as a simple .... We measure the .... change, then use the equation $Q = mc\Delta T$ to calculate the .... change.

2 A student added 50 cm³ of dilute hydrochloric acid to 50 cm³ of sodium hydroxide solution in a polystyrene calorimeter. She recorded a temperature rise of 11 °C.
   a Using $Q = mc\Delta T$, work out the energy change in her experiment. (Specific heat capacity of the solution is 4.2 J/g°C.)
   b There were 0.2 moles of both the acid and the alkali used. What would be the energy change in kJ per mole?

Key points

● We can calculate the energy change for reactions in solution by measuring the temperature change and using the equation:
$$Q = mc\Delta T$$
(The equation will be given in the exam)

● Neutralisation and displacement reactions are both examples of reactions that we can use this technique for.

C3 4.4   Titration calculations ⓚ

Learning objectives

- How can we calculate concentrations from reacting volumes?

- How can we calculate the amount of acid or alkali needed in a neutralisation reaction?

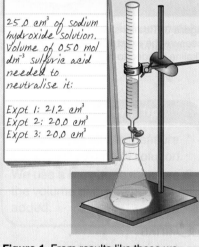

25.0 cm³ of sodium hydroxide solution. Volume of 0.50 mol dm³ sulfuric acid needed to neutralise it:

Expt 1: 21.2 cm³
Expt 2: 20.0 cm³
Expt 3: 20.0 cm³

Figure 1 From results like these we can work out the concentration of the unknown solution – in this case the sodium hydroxide solution

Calculating concentrations

The concentration of a solute in a solution is the number of moles of solute dissolved in one cubic decimetre of solution. We write these units as **moles per decimetre cubed** or **mol/dm³** for short. So if we know the mass of solute dissolved in a certain volume of solution, we can work out its concentration.

As an example, imagine that we make a solution of sodium hydroxide in water. We dissolve exactly 40 g of sodium hydroxide to make exactly 1 dm³ of solution. We know how to work out the mass of 1 mole of sodium hydroxide (NaOH). We add up the relative atomic masses of sodium, oxygen and hydrogen:

$$23 \,(Na) + 16 \,(O) + 1 \,(H) = 40\,g = \text{mass of 1 mole of NaOH}$$

Therefore we know that the solution contains 1 mole of sodium hydroxide in 1 dm³ of solution. So the concentration of sodium hydroxide in the solution is 1 mol/dm³. See Worked example 1.

🖩 *Maths skills*

Worked example 1

But what if we use 40 g of sodium hydroxide to make 500 cm³ of solution instead of 1 dm³? (Remember that 1 dm³ = 1000 cm³.)

Solution

To find the concentration of the solution we must work out how much sodium hydroxide there would be if we had 1000 cm³ (1 dm³) of the solution.

40 g of NaOH are dissolved in 500 cm³ of solution, so

$\dfrac{40}{500}$ g of NaOH would be dissolved in 1 cm³ of solution, and

$\dfrac{40}{500} \times 1000\,g = \textbf{80\,g}$ of NaOH would be dissolved in 1000 cm³ of solution.

The mass of 1 mole of NaOH is 40 g, so 80 g of NaOH is 80÷40 moles = **2 moles**.

2 moles of NaOH are dissolved in 1 dm³ of solution. So the concentration of NaOH in the solution is **2 mol/dm³**.

Sometimes we know the concentration of a solution and need to work out the mass of solute in a certain volume. See Worked example 2.

Titration calculations

In a titration we always have one solution with a concentration which we know accurately. We can put this in the burette. Then we can place the other solution, with an unknown concentration, in a conical flask. We do this using a pipette. This ensures we know the volume of this solution accurately. The result from the titration is used to calculate the number of moles of the substance in the solution in the conical flask. See Worked example 3.

Maths skills

Worked example 2

What mass of potassium sulfate, K_2SO_4, is there in 250 cm³ of a 1 mol/dm³ solution?

Solution

In 1 dm³ of solution there would be 1 mole of K_2SO_4

The mass of 1 mole of K_2SO_4 is $(2 \times 39) + 32 + (4 \times 16)$ g = 174 g, so

in 1000 cm³ of solution there would be 174 g of K_2SO_4, and

in 1 cm³ of solution there are $\dfrac{174}{1000}$ g of K_2SO_4

So in 250 cm³ of solution there are $\dfrac{174}{1000} \times 250$ g of K_2SO_4 = **43.5 g** of K_2SO_4

There is **43.5 g of K_2SO_4** in 250 cm³ of 1 mol/dm³ potassium sulfate solution.

Maths skills

Worked example 3

A student put 25.0 cm³ of sodium hydroxide solution of unknown concentration into a conical flask using a pipette. The sodium hydroxide reacted with exactly 20.0 cm³ of 0.50 mol/dm³ sulfuric acid added from a burette. What was the concentration of the sodium hydroxide solution?

Solution

The equation for this reaction is:

$2NaOH(aq) + H_2SO_4(aq) \rightarrow Na_2SO_4(aq) + 2H_2O(l)$

This equation tells us that 2 moles of NaOH reacts with 1 mole of H_2SO_4.

The concentration of the H_2SO_4 is 0.50 mol/dm³, so

0.50 moles of H_2SO_4 are dissolved in 1000 cm³ of acid, and

$\dfrac{0.50}{1000}$ moles of H_2SO_4 are dissolved in 1 cm³ of acid, therefore

$\dfrac{0.50}{1000} \times 20.0$ moles of H_2SO_4 are dissolved in 20.0 cm³ of acid.

So there are 0.010 moles of H_2SO_4 dissolved in 20.0 cm³ of acid.

The equation for the reaction tells us that 0.010 moles of H_2SO_4 will react with exactly 2×0.010 moles of NaOH. This means that there must have been 0.020 moles of NaOH in the 25.0 cm³ of solution in the conical flask. To calculate the concentration of NaOH in the solution in the flask we need to calculate the number of moles of NaOH in 1 dm³ (1000 cm³) of solution.

0.020 moles of NaOH are dissolved in 25.0 cm³ of solution, so

$\dfrac{0.020}{25}$ moles of NaOH are dissolved in 1 cm³ of solution, and there will be

$\dfrac{0.020}{25} \times 1000 = 0.80$ moles of NaOH in 1000 cm³ solution.

The concentration of the sodium hydroxide solution is 0.80 mol/dm³.

Summary questions

1 In a titration, a 25.0 cm³ sample of nitric acid (HNO_3) reacted exactly with 20.0 cm³ of 0.40 mol/dm³ sodium hydroxide solution.

   a Write down a balanced symbol equation for this reaction.

   b Calculate the number of moles of sodium hydroxide added.

   c Write down the number of moles of HNO_3 in the acid.

   d Calculate the concentration of the nitric acid.

Key points

- To calculate the concentration of a solution, given the mass of solute in a certain volume:

  1 Calculate the mass (in grams) of solute in 1 cm³ of solution.

  2 Calculate the mass (in grams) of solute in 1000 cm³ of solution.

  3 Convert the mass (in grams) to moles.

- To calculate the mass of solute in a certain volume of solution of known concentration:

  1 Calculate the mass (in grams) of the solute there is in 1 dm³ (1000 cm³) of solution.

  2 Calculate the mass (in grams) of solute in 1 cm³ of solution.

  3 Calculate the mass (in grams) of solute there is in the given volume of the solution.

C3 5.2

Properties and uses of alcohols k

Learning objectives

- What are the properties of alcohols?
- What are the main uses of alcohols?
- What is produced when ethanol is fully oxidised?

⊂⊃ links

For more information on the production of ethanol and its use as a fuel, look back to C1 5.5 Ethanol.

⊂⊃ links

For information on the dangers of drinking ethanol, see C3 5.4 Organic issues.

Figure 1 Alcohols are used as solvents in perfumes

?!? Did you know ... ?

Ethanol is the main solvent in many perfumes but a key ingredient in some perfumes is octanol. It evaporates more slowly and so holds the perfume on the skin for longer.

Alcohols, especially ethanol, are commonly used in everyday products. We have already seen how ethanol is the main alcohol we refer to in alcoholic drinks. This is made by fermenting sugars from plant material. It is becoming an important alternative fuel to petrol and diesel. We also saw how ethanol can be made from ethene and steam in industry.

a What is the main alcohol in alcoholic drinks?

Alcohols dissolve many of the same substances as water. In fact the alcohols with smaller molecules mix very well with water, giving neutral solutions. The alcohols can also dissolve many other organic compounds. This property makes them useful as solvents. For example, we can remove ink stains from permanent marker pens using methylated spirits.

Methylated spirits ('meths') is mainly ethanol but has the more toxic methanol mixed with it. It also has a purple dye added and other substances to make it unpleasant to drink. Alcohols are also used as solvents in products such as perfumes, aftershaves and mouthwashes.

Reactions of alcohols

Practical/Demonstration

Comparing the reactions of methanol, ethanol and propanol

a Ignite and observe the flame in three spirit burners – one containing methanol, one ethanol and the other propanol.
- Compare the three combustion reactions.

b Watch your teacher add a small piece of sodium metal to each of the alcohols.
- Compare the reactions. Which gas is given off?

c Watch your teacher boil some of each alcohol with acidified potassium dichromate(VI) solution.
- What do you see happen in each reaction?

Combustion

The use of ethanol (and also methanol) as fuels shows that the alcohols are flammable. Ethanol is used in spirit burners. It burns with a 'clean' blue flame:

$$\text{ethanol} + \text{oxygen} \rightarrow \text{carbon dioxide} + \text{water}$$
$$C_2H_5OH + 3O_2 \rightarrow 2CO_2 + 3H_2O$$

Reaction with sodium

The alcohols react in a similar way to water when sodium is added. The sodium fizzes, giving off hydrogen gas, and dissolves away to form a solution. Their reactions are not as vigorous as the reaction we observe with water.

Oxidation

Combustion is one way to oxidise an alcohol. However, when we use chemical oxidising agents, such as potassium dichromate(VI), we get different products. An alcohol is oxidised to a carboxylic acid when boiled with acidified potassium dichromate(VI) solution.

> **b** Is potassium dichromate(VI) a reducing agent or an oxidising agent?

So ethanol can be oxidised to ethanoic acid. The same reaction takes place if ethanol is left exposed to air. Microbes in the air produce ethanoic acid from the ethanol. That's why bottles of beer or wine taste and smell like vinegar when they are left open.

Figure 2 Alcohols are flammable. They produce carbon dioxide and water in their combustion reactions.

Practical

Oxidation by microbes in air

Add 5 cm³ of ethanol to 50 cm³ of water in a conical flask, mix and test the pH of the solution formed.

Then mix 5 cm³ of ethanol with 50 cm³ of water in a second conical flask but this time seal the flask with a stopper.

Leave both solutions for a few weeks, swirling occasionally.

- What happens to the pH of the solutions?
- Explain your observations.

Summary questions

1 Copy and complete using the words below:

hydrogen ethanoic water carbon carboxylic neutral microbes

Methanol, ethanol and propanol all dissolve in water to form a .... solution. The alcohols react with sodium metal, with the sodium fizzing to produce .... gas. When they burn in air, they form .... dioxide and .... as the products of combustion. They are also oxidised by acidified potassium dichromate(VI) solution to form .... acids.

The ethanol in alcoholic drinks is oxidised to .... acid by .... if left exposed to the air.

2 List the main uses of alcohols.

3 Plan an investigation to see which alcohol – methanol, ethanol or propanol – releases most energy per gram when it burns.

Key points

- Alcohols are used as solvents and fuels, and ethanol is the main alcohol in alcoholic drinks.

- Alcohols burn in air, forming carbon dioxide and water.

- With sodium metal, alcohols react to form a solution, and hydrogen gas is given off.

- Ethanol can be oxidised to ethanoic acid, either by chemical oxidising agents or by the action of microbes. Ethanoic acid is the main acid in vinegar.

C3 5.3

Carboxylic acids and esters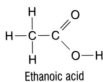

Learning objectives

- How can we recognise carboxylic acids from their properties?
- What do we use carboxylic acids and esters for?
- Why are carboxylic acids described as weak acids? [H]
- How can we make esters?

⚲ links

For more information on the structure of carboxylic acids, see C3 5.1 Structures of alcohols, carboxylic acids and esters.

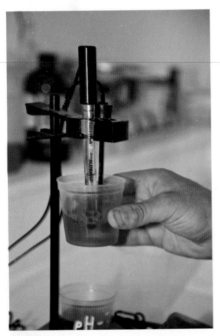

Figure 2 Testing the pH of a solution using a pH sensor

You have already learned about the structure of carboxylic acids. The most well-known carboxylic acid is ethanoic acid.

Ethanoic acid

Figure 1 Ethanoic acid, CH_3COOH, is the main acid in vinegar. Its old name was 'acetic acid'. Carboxylic acids are also used to make polyester fibres.

Carboxylic acids, as their name suggests, form acidic solutions when they dissolve in water. You can look at their reactions in the next experiment.

Practical

Comparing ethanoic acid and hydrochloric acid

Write down your observations to compare ethanoic acid with hydrochloric acid of the same concentration.

a Take the pH of solutions of both acids.

b Add a little sodium carbonate to solutions of both acids.

- Why did we use the same concentrations of each acid in the experiment?

Carboxylic acids still have the typical reactions of all acids. For example:

ethanoic + sodium → sodium + water + carbon dioxide
acid   carbonate   ethanoate

a Which gas is made when propanoic acid reacts with potassium carbonate?

Why are carboxylic acids called 'weak acids'?

You have seen how CO_2 gas is given off more slowly when a carbonate reacts with a carboxylic acid than with hydrochloric acid of the same concentration. Carboxylic acids are called **weak** acids, as opposed to **strong** acids such as hydrochloric acid.

The pH of a 0.1 mol/dm³ solution of hydrochloric acid (a strong acid) is 1.0. Yet a 0.1 mol/dm³ solution of ethanoic acid (a weak acid) has a higher pH of 2.9. The solution of ethanoic acid is not as acidic even though the two solutions have the same concentration. Why is this?

Acids must dissolve in water before they show their acidic properties. That is because in water all acids ionise. Their molecules split up to form a negative ion and $H^+(aq)$ ions. It is the $H^+(aq)$ ions that all acidic solutions have in common. For example, in hydrochloric acid, the HCl molecules all ionise in water:

$$HCl(aq) \xrightarrow{\text{water}} H^+(aq) + Cl^-(aq)$$

Higher

Higher

We say that strong acids ionise *completely* in solution. However, in weak acids most of the molecules stay as they are. Only some will ionise (split up) in their solutions. A position of equilibrium is reached in which the molecules and ions are all present. So in ethanoic acid we get:

$$CH_3COOH(aq) \rightleftharpoons CH_3COO^-(aq) + H^+(aq)$$

Therefore given two aqueous solutions of equal concentration, the strong acid will have a higher concentration of $H^+(aq)$ ions than the solution of the weak acid. So a weak acid has a higher pH (and reacts more slowly with a carbonate).

Making esters

Carboxylic acids also react with alcohols to make esters. Water is also formed in this reversible reaction. An acid, usually sulfuric acid, is used as a catalyst. For example:

$$\text{ethanoic acid} + \text{ethanol} \xrightarrow[\text{sulfuric acid catalyst}]{} \text{ethyl ethanoate} + \text{water}$$
$$(CH_3COOC_2H_5)$$

In general:

$$\textbf{carboxylic acid} + \textbf{alcohol} \xrightarrow[\text{strong acid catalyst}]{} \textbf{ester} + \textbf{water}$$

Here is another example:

ethanoic acid + **methanol** ⇌ **methyl ethanoate** + water

The esters formed have distinctive smells. They are volatile (evaporate easily). Many smell sweet and fruity. This makes them ideal to use in perfumes and food flavourings.

> **b** Name the ester formed from ethanoic acid and ethanol.
> **c** Esters are volatile compounds. What does this mean?

Demonstration

Making esters

Your teacher will show you how to make different esters using carboxylic acids and alcohols.

After neutralising the acid with sodium hydrogencarbonate, carefully smell the test tubes containing the different esters formed.

● Write word equations for each reaction.

Key points

● Solutions of carboxylic acids have a pH value less than 7. Carbonates gently fizz in their acidic solutions, releasing carbon dioxide gas.

● Aqueous solutions of weak acids have a higher pH value than solutions of strong acids with the same concentration. **[H]**

● Esters are made by reacting a carboxylic acid and an alcohol together with an acid catalyst.

● Esters are volatile compounds used in flavourings and perfumes.

Summary questions

1 Copy and complete using the words below:

reversible volatile alcohols perfumes sulfuric carbonates water

Carboxylic acids react with ...., giving off carbon dioxide gas.

Carboxylic acids also react with .... to form esters and .... This .... reaction is catalysed by .... acid. The esters formed are .... compounds used in flavourings and ....

2 Write a word equation to show the reversible reaction between methanoic acid and ethanol.

3 Explain why propanoic acid is described as a weak acid.   **[H]**

C3 5.4

Organic issues

Ethanol in drinks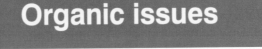

An alcoholic drink, such as one glass of red wine, can help people relax. It can help relieve the stress for some people after a hard day at work. However, too many people are drinking more than the maximum recommended amount of alcohol. This puts their health at risk. Alcohol has been associated with high blood pressure and heart disease. Excess alcohol can also damage the liver. In extreme cases, a liver transplant is the only way to avoid death.

Alcohol is a socially acceptable drug. Like other drugs, some people become dependent on it. Alcoholics are addicted to ethanol. Many ruin their lives because their behaviour changes as a result of drinking alcohol.

Ethanol is used in methylated spirits as a solvent. Some desperate addicts will drink this because it contains a lot of ethanol and it's cheap. They will do this even though it has had toxic methanol added to it. It also contains emetics (substances that make you vomit) and foul-tasting chemicals.

Drinking 'meths' causes liver failure, blindness and an early death. Other chemicals are also added to methylated spirits to make it more difficult to distil off the ethanol. By including chemicals with similar boiling points, people can't separate off the ethanol for drinking.

a Why is it very difficult to distil ethanol from methylated spirits?

Alcoholic drinks are more expensive than methylated spirits because they have tax added on. The government can use the income generated for many good causes. However, we should weigh this against the costs of dealing with:

- the health problems
- days lost at work
- policing antisocial behaviour.

Learning objectives

- What are the issues involved in the use of alcohols, carboxylic acids and esters?

Figure 1 Addiction to alcohol can cause many problems for the individuals themselves and society as a whole

∞ links

For more information on the use of ethanol as a solvent in methylated spirits, see C3 5.2 Properties and uses of alcohols.

??? Did you know ...?

When European winemakers produce more wine than they can sell, it is distilled to make ethanol for industrial purposes (not for alcoholic drinks).

Figure 2 Binge drinking can cause violent behaviour. In severe cases it leads to alcoholic poisoning. Doctors are reporting an increasing number of alcohol-related health problems in 20- to 30-year-olds. These problems used to be seen mainly in middle-aged alcoholics.

links

For more information on using ethanol as a biofuel and vegetable oils for making biodiesel, look back to C1 4.5 Alternative fuels.

Activity

Raising the cost of alcoholic drinks?

Some people are campaigning against the sale of cheap alcoholic drinks in supermarkets. They argue that it makes alcohol more easily available, especially to young adults. Cheap promotions in bars are also criticised for encouraging excessive drinking.

● Make a table with points for and against the banning of cheap alcoholic drinks in supermarkets and 'happy hours' in bars.

Ethanol and esters as biofuels

You have seen that ethanol can be used as a biofuel. It is made by fermenting sugars from crops. We also looked at biodiesel. This is made from plant oils which are esters. In processing these esters, the oils are broken down into long-chain carboxylic acids. They are then reacted with methanol or ethanol (in the presence of a catalyst) to make the esters used as biodiesel.

b Which alcohol is used to make an ethyl ester used as biodiesel?

However, the land used for biofuel crops could be used for food crops. With an ever-increasing world population, feeding ourselves will become more of an issue. We will need more land for farming – both for fuels and food.

This new farming land is often made by cutting down and burning tropical rainforests. This destroys habitats of wildlife and contributes towards increasing the percentage of carbon dioxide in the atmosphere. Yet alternatives to crude oil are needed urgently, so what can we do?

Activity

The way ahead

Work as a small group to make a list of ideas for a new government to help deal with the fuel crisis facing us.

Present your ideas to the rest of the class and arrive at a single list together.

??? Did you know ... ?

You can buy this machine to make your own biodiesel at home. It can produce up to 50 litres a day from a mixture of used or new cooking oils and methanol.

Figure 3 A domestic biodiesel generator

Key points

● Alcohols, carboxylic acids and esters have many uses which benefit society.

● Some of these substances, such as ethanol and solvents, can be abused.

● In future, the use of biofuels, such as ethanol and esters, could help society as crude oil supplies run out.

● Future uses of biofuels might conflict with the need to feed the world.

Summary questions

1 **a** What are the social affects of drinking alcohol and driving?
   b Some people would prefer it to be illegal to have any trace of alcohol in the blood at all when driving. At present you must have more than 80 mg of alcohol per 100 cm³ of blood in order to be prosecuted. What might be a difficulty with a limit of 0 mg of ethanol?

2 If more and more farmers grow crops for biofuels, what could happen to the price of crop-based foods such as bread? How might this become a cyclical problem which gets worse and then better at regular intervals?

Summary questions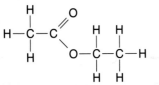

1 Look at the three organic molecules A, B and C below:

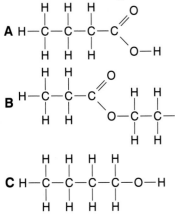

Answer these questions about **A**, **B** and **C**:

a Which one is a carboxylic acid?

b Which one is an alcohol?

c Which homologous series of organic compounds does B belong to?

d Which of the compounds can be represented as $CH_3CH_2COOCH_2CH_3$?

e Using a structural formula as shown in part **d**, give the structural formulae of the other two compounds.

2 a Describe what you would see happen if a small piece of sodium metal was dropped into a beaker containing some ethanol.

b Name the gas given off in the reaction described in part **a**.

3 a Draw the displayed formula of propanoic acid, showing all the atoms and bonds.

b Some calcium carbonate powder is dropped into a test tube of a solution of propanoic acid. How would you positively identify the gas given off?

4 a What is the name of this compound?

b Write a word equation showing how this compound can be made. Include the catalyst.

c The compound shown is volatile. What can you say about its boiling point?

d Name the carboxylic acid and the alcohol we would use to make propyl methanoate.

5 State one use of:

a alcohols

b carboxylic acids

c esters.

6 Describe how could you distinguish between samples of ethanol, ethanoic acid and ethyl ethanoate using simple tests.

7 Propanol was burned in a spirit burner and the products of combustion were tested as shown below:

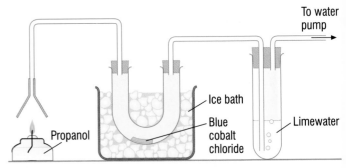

a In the style of Question **1 d**, write the structural formula of propanol.

b After the propanol has been burning for a while, what happens in:
   i   the U-tube
   ii the boiling tube containing limewater?

c What does this experiment show?

d Write a word equation to show the combustion of propanol.

e Write a balanced symbol equation to show the combustion of propanol. **[H]**

8 You are given a 0.1 mol/dm³ solution of nitric acid, and a solution of propanoic acid with the same concentration.

a What can you predict about the pH of the two solutions? **[H]**

b Explain your answer to part **a**. **[H]**

AQA Examination-style questions 🅚

1 The displayed formula of a compound is

```
   H   H
   |   |
H—C—C—O—H
   |   |
   H   H
```

Choose an answer from the lists to complete each sentence.

a This compound is called .... (1)

methanol   ethanol   propanol

b The structural formula of this compound is .... (1)

CH₃CH₂OH   CH₃COOH   CH₃COOCH₃

c The functional group in this compound is .... (1)

–COOH   –OH   –COO–

2 The structural formulae of three substances A, B and C are shown.

CH₃CH₂COOH   CH₃COOCH₂CH₃   CH₃CH₂CH₂OH
    A   **B**   **C**

a Match each substance with the group of compounds to which it belongs.

  i   alcohol
  ii   carboxylic acid
  iii   ester (1)

b Which substance is called ethyl ethanoate? (1)

c Which substance has the formula $C_3H_6O_2$? (1)

3 A technician found three bottles of liquids on a shelf. The labels had fallen off. The labels were ethanol, ethanoic acid and ethyl ethanoate. The technician wrote A, B and C on the three bottles and tested the liquids. The technician's results are shown in the table.

Test	Results		
	A	**B**	**C**
Add a few drops of liquid to 2 cm³ of water and add Universal Indicator.	red	green	green
Add a few drops of sodium carbonate solution to 2 cm³ of liquid.	fizzed	no reaction	no reaction
Add a small piece of sodium to 2 cm³ of liquid	not tested	fizzed	no reaction

Match the labels with the liquids A, B and C, giving reasons for your conclusions. (4)

4 Methylated spirits is a mixture of ethanol with 5 to 10% methanol. Methanol is much more toxic than ethanol. Methylated spirits is used as a fuel for spirit burners and as a solvent for cleaning and decorating.
The equation for the complete combustion of ethanol is:

$CH_3CH_2OH + 3O_2 \rightarrow 2CO_2 + 3H_2O$

a **i** Write a word equation for the complete combustion of methanol. (1)
  ii Suggest **two** reasons why methylated spirits is suitable for use as a fuel in spirit burners used as camping stoves. (2)

b **i** What is the structural formula of methanol? (1)
  ii Explain why methanol mixes completely with ethanol. (2)

c Methylated spirits can be used to clean glass windows and mirrors. Suggest **two** properties that make it suitable for cleaning glass. (2)

d Methylated spirits containing 90 to 95% ethanol costs much less than vodka containing 40% ethanol. This is because alcohol sold in the UK for drinking is taxed at a high rate by the UK government.
  i Suggest **one** reason why the UK government tax alcohol for drinking at a high rate. (1)
  ii Why is methylated spirits not taxed at the same rate? (1)

5 **a** The flavour and smell of wine that is kept in bottles for some time may improve.

One of the reactions that may take place is:

$CH_3COOH + CH_3CH_2OH \rightarrow CH_3COOCH_2CH_3 + H_2O$
Explain why this reaction would improve the smell of the wine. (2)

b Beer contains about 5% ethanol. Explain why beer that is left exposed to the air for several hours tastes sour. (3)

6 Sulfuric acid ionises completely when dissolved in water.

a Balance the equation that shows what happens to sulfuric acid in water.

$H_2SO_4(aq) \rightarrow H^+(aq) + SO_4^{2-}(aq)$ [H] (1)

b Write a balanced symbol equation to show what happens when ethanoic acid, CH_3COOH, is dissolved in water. [H] (2)

c You have been given two solutions of acids with the same concentration. One is ethanoic acid, the other is sulfuric acid. Describe and give the results of a test that you could use to show which acid is in each solution. Explain the results of your test. [H] (5)

1 The diagram shows a simplified flow diagram of a water treatment works which
   supplies drinking water.

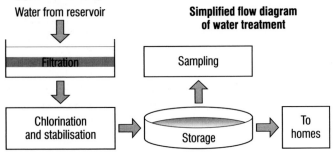

a i   What is the purpose of filtration?   (1)
  ii   What is the purpose of chlorination?   (1)
b Samples of the treated water must be tested at regular intervals. Suggest one reason
   why.   (1)
c In some parts of the country the water supplied to homes is hard water.
   i   Name **one** ion that can make water hard.   (1)
   ii   Explain how hard water can affect central heating systems.   (3)
   iii State **one** advantage of hard water.   (1)

                                                                   AQA, 2007

2 Ethanol can be used as a fuel. The equation for the combustion of ethanol is:

$$CH_3CH_2OH + 3O_2 \rightarrow 2CO_2 + 3H_2O$$

Use the energy level diagram to help you answer these questions.

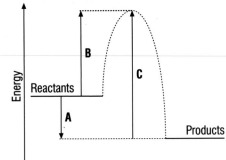

a How can you tell from the diagram that this reaction is exothermic?   (1)
b Copy the diagram and draw a line to show what happens if a catalyst is used. (1)
c What is the effect of a catalyst on the overall energy change for the reaction? (1)

The student decided to calculate the energy change using bond energies. He wrote this
equation to help.

$$\underset{\substack{| \ \ | \\ H \ H}}{H-\underset{\substack{| \\ H}}{\overset{\substack{H \\ |}}{C}}-\underset{\substack{| \\ H}}{\overset{\substack{H \\ |}}{C}}-O-H} + 3[O=O] \longrightarrow 2[O=C=O] + 3[H-O-H]$$

He looked up the following bond energies.

Bond	Bond energy in kJ per mole	Bond	Bond energy in kJ per mole
C—H	413	O—H	464
C—C	347	O=O	498
C—O	336	C=O	805

d Calculate the energy needed to break the bonds in the reactants.   [H] (3)
e Calculate the energy released when the bonds in the products are formed.   [H] (2)
f Calculate the energy change for the reaction.   [H] (1)
g Calculate the energy change in joules per g of ethanol.   [H] (2)

AQA *Examiner's tip*

In questions that ask you
to explain, such as **Q1 c ii**,
you must link the points
logically and coherently in
your answer. This means
you should use words like
'because' and 'therefore' in
your explanation.

3 Some chemical tests were done on solutions of four substances, A, B, C and D. The table shows the tests and the results of the tests.

Substance	Flame test colour	Sodium hydroxide solution added	Nitric acid and silver nitrate solution added	Hydrochloric acid and barium chloride added
A	No colour	White precipitate that dissolves in excess sodium hydroxide	No reaction	White precipitate
B	Lilac	No reaction	Cream precipitate	No reaction
C	Crimson	No reaction	White precipitate	No reaction
D	No colour	Green precipitate	No reaction	White precipitate

Name the four substances A, B, C and D. (8)

4 When compound X with the formula $CH_3COOCH_2CH_3$ is heated with dilute hydrochloric acid it reacts with water. Two compounds Y and Z are produced. The equation for the reaction is:

$$CH_3COOCH_2CH_3 + H_2O \rightarrow CH_3COOH + CH_3CH_2OH$$
$$\quad\quad\;\textbf{X}\quad\quad\quad\quad\quad\quad\quad\quad\quad\;\textbf{Y}\quad\quad\quad\quad\;\textbf{Z}$$

a Name compounds X, Y and Z. (3)

b For each of X, Y and Z, name the group of organic compounds to which it belongs. (3)

c Y and Z can be separated by distillation. They are both colourless liquids. Describe a simple test that you could use to distinguish between Y and Z. Give the results of the test for both Y and Z. (3)

5 *In this question you will be assessed for using good English, organising information clearly and using specialist terms where appropriate.*

Ammonia is produced by the Haber process. In the process nitrogen and hydrogen are mixed. The pressure is increased to about 200 atmospheres. The gases are passed over an iron catalyst at about 450 °C. The equation for the reaction is:

$$N_2(g) + 3H_2(g) \rightleftharpoons 2NH_3(g)$$

The reaction between nitrogen and hydrogen is reversible. This affects the amount of ammonia that it is possible to obtain from the process. The graph shows how the pressure and temperature affect the percentage of ammonia that can be produced.

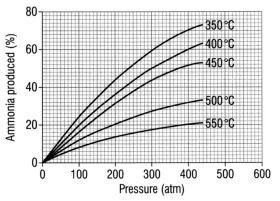

Use this information, together with your knowledge of the process, to explain why many industrial ammonia plants operate at 200 atmospheres and 450 °C. [H] (6)

AQA, 2006

Glossary

A

Accurate A measurement is considered accurate if it is judged to be close to the true value.

Acid A sour substance which can attack metal, clothing or skin. The chemical opposite of an alkali. When dissolved in water, its solution has a pH number less than 7. Acids are proton (H^+ ion) donors.

Activation energy The minimum energy needed to start off a reaction.

Alkali Its solution has a pH number more than 7.

Alkali metal Elements in Group 1 of the periodic table, e.g. lithium (Li), sodium (Na), potassium (K).

Alkane Saturated hydrocarbon with the general formula C_nH_{2n+2}, e.g. methane, ethane and propane.

Alkene Unsaturated hydrocarbon which contains a carbon–carbon double bond. Its general formula is C_nH_{2n}, e.g. ethene C_2H_4.

Alloy A mixture of metals (and sometimes non-metals). For example, brass is a mixture of copper and zinc.

Aluminium A low density, corrosion-resistant metal used in many alloys, including those used in the aircraft industry.

Anhydrous Describes a substance that does not contain water.

Anomalous results Results that do not match the pattern seen in the other data collected or are well outside the range of other repeat readings. They should be retested and if necessary discarded.

Aqueous solution The mixture made by adding a soluble substance to water.

Atmosphere The relatively thin layer of gases that surround planet Earth.

Atom The smallest part of an element that can still be recognised as that element.

Atomic number The number of protons (which equals the number of electrons) in an atom. It is sometimes called the proton number.

B

Bar chart A chart with rectangular bars with lengths proportional to the values that they represent. The bars should be of equal width and are usually plotted horizontally or vertically. Also called a bar graph.

Base The oxide, hydroxide or carbonate of a metal that will react with an acid, forming a salt as one of the products. (If a base dissolves in water it is called an alkali). Bases are proton (H^+ ion) acceptors.

Biodegradable Materials that can be broken down by microorganisms.

Biodiesel Fuel for cars made from plant oils.

Biofuel Fuel made from animal or plant products.

Bioleaching Process of extraction of metals from ores using microorganisms.

Blast furnace The huge reaction vessels used in industry to extract iron from its ore.

Bond energy The energy needed to break a particular chemical bond.

Brine A solution of sodium chloride in water.

Burette A long glass tube with a tap at one end and markings to show volumes of liquid, used to add precisely known amounts of liquids to a solution in a conical flask below it.

C

Calcium carbonate The main compound found in limestone. It is a white solid whose formula is $CaCO_3$.

Calcium hydroxide A white solid made by reacting calcium oxide with water. It is used as a cheap alkali in industry.

Calcium oxide A white solid made by heating limestone strongly, e.g. in a lime kiln.

Carbon monoxide A toxic gas whose formula is CO.

Carbon steel Alloy of iron containing controlled, small amounts of carbon.

Cast iron The impure iron taken directly from a blast furnace.

Catalyst A substance that speeds up a chemical reaction but remains chemically unchanged itself at the end of the reaction.

Catalytic converter Fitted to exhausts of vehicles to reduce pollutants released.

Cement A building material made by heating limestone and clay.

Chromatography The process whereby small amounts of dissolved substances are separated by running a solvent along a material such as absorbent paper.

Collision theory An explanation of chemical reactions in terms of reacting particles colliding with sufficient energy for a reaction to take place.

Compound A substance made when two or more elements are chemically bonded together. For example, water (H_2O) is a compound made from hydrogen and oxygen.

Concrete A building material made by mixing cement, sand and aggregate (crushed rock) with water.

Control group If an experiment is to determine the effect of changing a single variable, a control is often set up in which the independent variable is not changed, thus enabling a comparison to be made. If the investigation is of the survey type a control group is usually established to serve the same purpose.

Convection currents The circular motion of matter caused by heating in fluids.

Copper-rich ore Rock that contains a high proportion of a copper compound.

Core The centre of the Earth.

Covalent bond The attraction between two atoms that share one or more pairs of electrons.

Covalent bonding The attraction between two atoms that share one or more pairs of electrons.

Cracking The reaction used in the oil industry to break down large hydrocarbons into smaller, more useful ones. This occurs when the hydrocarbon vapour is either passed over a hot catalyst or mixed with steam and heated to a high temperature.

Crust The outer solid layer of the Earth.

D

Data Information, either qualitative or quantitative, that have been collected.

Delocalised electron Bonding electron that is no longer associated with any one particular atom.

Directly proportional A relationship that, when drawn on a line graph, shows a positive linear relationship that crosses through the origin.

Displace When one element takes the place of another in a compound. For example: iron + copper sulfate → iron sulfate + copper

Distillation Separation of a liquid from a mixture by evaporation followed by condensation.

Dot and cross diagram A drawing to show the arrangement of the outer shell electrons only of the atoms or ions in a substance.

Double bond A covalent bond made by the sharing of two pairs of electrons.

E

E number Number assigned to a food additive that has been approved for use in Europe. It is displayed on food packaging.

Electrolysis The breakdown of a substance containing ions by electricity.

Electrolyte A liquid, containing free-moving ions, that is broken down by electricity in the process of electrolysis.

Electron A tiny particle with a negative charge. Electrons orbit the nucleus in atoms or ions.

Electronic structure A set of numbers to show the arrangement of electrons in their shells (or energy levels), e.g. the electronic structure of a potassium atom is 2, 8, 8, 1.

Electroplating The process of depositing a thin layer of metal on an object during electrolysis.

Element A substance made up of only one type of atom. An element cannot be broken down chemically into any simpler substance.

Empirical formula The simplest ratio of elements in a compound.

Emulsifier A substance which helps keep immiscible liquids (e.g. oil and water) mixed so that they do not separate out into layers.

Emulsion A mixture of liquids that do not dissolve in each other.

Endothermic A reaction that *takes in* energy from the surroundings.

End point The point in a titration where the reaction is complete and titration should stop.

Energy level see Shell.

Equilibrium The point in a reversible reaction in which the forward and backward rates of reaction are the same. Therefore, the amounts of substances present in the reacting mixture remain constant.

Error Sometimes called an uncertainty.

Error – human Often present in the collection of data, and may be random or systematic. For example, the effect of human reaction time when recording short time intervals with a stopwatch.

Error – random Causes readings to be spread about the true value, due to results varying in an unpredictable way from one measurement to the next. Random errors are present when any measurement is made, and cannot be corrected. The effect of random errors can be reduced by making more measurements and calculating a new mean.

Error – systematic Causes readings to be spread about some value other than the true value, due to results differing from the true value by a consistent amount each time a measurement is made. Sources of systematic error can include the environment, methods of observation or instruments used. Systematic errors cannot be dealt with by simple repeats. If a systematic error is suspected, the data collection should be repeated using a different technique or a different set of equipment, and the results compared.

Error – zero Any indication that a measuring system gives a false reading when the true value of a measured quantity is zero, for example, the needle on an ammeter failing to return to zero when no current flows.

Ethene An alkene with the formula C_2H_4.

Evidence Data which have been shown to be valid.

Exothermic A reaction that *gives out* energy to the surroundings.

F

Fair test A fair test is one in which only the independent variable has been allowed to affect the dependent variable.

Fermentation The reaction in which the enzymes in yeast turn glucose into ethanol and carbon dioxide.

Flammable Easily ignited and capable of burning rapidly.

Food additive A substance added to a food in order to preserve it or to improve its taste, texture or appearance.

Fraction Hydrocarbons with similar boiling points separated from crude oil.

Fractional distillation A way to separate liquids from a mixture of liquids by boiling off the substances at different temperatures, then condensing and collecting the liquids.

Fullerene Form of the element carbon that can form a large cage-like structure, based on hexagonal rings of carbon atoms.

Functional group An atom or group of atoms that give organic compounds their characteristic reactions.

G

Gas A state of matter.

Gas chromatography The process of separating the components in a mixture by passing the vapours through a column and detecting them as they leave the column at different times.

Giant covalent structure A huge 3D network of covalently bonded atoms (e.g. the giant lattice of carbon atoms in diamond or graphite).

Giant lattice A huge 3D network of atoms or ions (e.g. the giant ionic lattice in sodium chloride).

Giant structure See Giant lattice.

Global dimming The reflection of sunlight by tiny solid particles in the air.

Global warming The increasing of the average temperature of the Earth.

Group All the elements in each column (labelled 1 to 7 and 0) down the periodic table.

H

Half equation An equation that describes reduction (gain of electrons) or oxidation (loss of electrons), such as the reactions that take place at the electrodes during electrolysis. For example: $Na^+ + e^- \rightarrow Na$.

Hardening The process of reacting plant oils with hydrogen to raise their melting point. This is used to make spreadable margarine.

Hard water Water in which it is difficult to form a lather with soap. It contains calcium and/or magnesium ions which react with soap to produce scum.

Hazard A hazard is something (for example, an object, a property of a substance or an activity) that can cause harm.

High-alloy steel Expensive alloy of iron mixed with relatively large proportions of other metals e.g. stainless steel which contains nickel and chromium along with the iron.

Homologous series A group of related organic compounds that have the same functional group, e.g. the molecules of the homologous series of alcohols all contain the –OH group.

Hydrated Describes a substance that contains water in its crystals, e.g. hydrated copper sulfate.

Hydration A reaction in which water (H_2O) is chemically added to a compound.

Hydrocarbon A compound containing only hydrogen and carbon.

Hydrogenated oil Oil which has had hydrogen added to it to reduce its degree of saturation in the hardening process to make margarine.

Hydrophilic The water-loving part of an emulsifier molecule.

Hydrophobic The water-hating hydrocarbon part of an emulsifier molecule.

Hypothesis A proposal intended to explain certain facts or observations.

I

Incomplete combustion When a fuel burns in insufficient oxygen, producing carbon monoxide as a toxic product.

Inert Unreactive.

Intermolecular forces The attraction between the individual molecules in a covalently bonded substance.

Interval The quantity between readings, for example, a set of 11 readings equally spaced over a distance of 1 m would give an interval of 10 cm.

Ion A charged particle produced by the loss or gain of electrons.

Ion-exchange column A water softener which works by replacing calcium and magnesium ions with sodium or hydrogen ions, removing the hardness.

Ionic bond The electrostatic force of attraction between positively and negatively charged ions.

Ionic bonding The electrostatic force of attraction between positively and negatively charged ions.

Isotope Atom that has the same number of protons but different number of neutrons, i.e. it has the same atomic number but different mass number.

L

Limewater The common name for calcium hydroxide solution.

Line graph Used when both variables are continuous. The line should normally be a line of best fit, and may be straight or a smooth curve. (Exceptionally, in some (mainly biological) investigations, the line may be a 'point-to-point' line.)

Liquid A state of matter.

Low-alloy steel Alloy of iron containing small amounts (1–5 per cent) of other metals.

M

Macromolecule Giant covalent structure.

Mantle The layer of the Earth between its crust and its core.

Mass number The number of protons plus neutrons in the nucleus of an atom.

Mass spectrometer A machine that can be used to analyse small amounts of a substance to identify it and to find its relative molecular mass.

Mean The arithmetical average of a series of numbers.

Mixture When some elements or compounds are mixed together and intermingle but do not react together (i.e. no new substance is made). A mixture is *not* a pure substance.

Mole The amount of substance in the relative atomic or formula mass of a substance in grams.

Molecular formula The chemical formula that shows the actual numbers of atoms in a particular molecule (e.g. C_2H_4).

Molecular ion peak The peak on the mass spectrum of a substance which tells us the relative molecular mass of the substance. The peak is produced by the heaviest positive ion shown on the mass spectrum.

Molecule A group of atoms bonded together e.g. PCl_5.

Monitor Observations made over a period of time.

Monomers Small reactive molecules that react together in repeating sequences to form a very large molecule (a polymer).

Mortar A building material used to bind bricks together. It is made by mixing cement and sand with water.

N

Nanoscience The study of very tiny particles or structures between 1 and 100 nanometres in size – where 1 nanometre = 10.9 metres.

Neutral A solution with a pH value of 7 which is neither acidic nor an alkaline. Alternatively, something that carries no overall electrical charge – neither positively nor negatively charged.

Neutralisation The chemical reaction of an acid with a base in which they cancel each other out, forming a salt and water. If the base is a carbonate or hydrogen carbonate, carbon dioxide is also produced in the reaction.

Neutron A dense particle found in the nucleus of an atom. It is electrically neutral, carrying no charge.

Nitrogen oxide Gaseous pollutant given off from motor vehicles, a cause of acid rain.

Non-renewable Something which cannot be replaced once it is used up.

Nucleus (of an atom) The very small and dense central part of an atom which contains protons and neutrons.

O

Opinion A belief not backed up by facts or evidence.

Ore Ore is rock which contains enough metal to make it economically worthwhile to extract the metal.

Oxidation The reaction when oxygen is added to a substance (or when electrons are lost).

Oxidised A reaction where oxygen is added to a substance (or when electrons are lost from a substance).

P

Particulate Small solid particle given off from motor vehicles as a result of incomplete combustion of its fuel.

Percentage yield The actual mass of product collected in a reaction divided by the maximum mass that could have been formed in theory, multiplied by 100.

Periodic table An arrangement of elements in the order of their atomic numbers, forming groups and periods.

Permanent hard water Hard water whose calcium and/or magnesium ions are not removed when the water is boiled, thus remaining hard.

pH scale A number which shows how strongly acidic or alkaline a solution is. Acids have a pH value of less than 7 (pH 1 is strongly acidic). Alkalis have a pH value above 7 (pH 14 is strongly alkaline). A neutral liquid has a pH value of 7.

Phytomining The process of extraction of metals from ores using plants.

Pipette A glass tube used to measure accurate volumes of liquids.

Polymer A substance made from very large molecules made up of many repeating units e.g. poly(ethene).

Polymerisation The reaction of monomers to make a polymer.

Precipitate An insoluble solid formed by a reaction taking place in solution.

Precise A precise measurement is one in which there is very little spread about the mean value. Precision depends only on the extent of random errors – it gives no indication of how close results are to the true value.

Precision A precise set of repeat readings will be closely grouped together.

Prediction A forecast or statement about the way something will happen in the future. In science it is not just a simple guess, because it is based on some prior knowledge or on a hypothesis.

Product A substance made as a result of a chemical reaction.

Propene An alkene with the formula C_3H_6.

Proton A tiny positive particle found inside the nucleus of an atom.

R

Range The maximum and minimum values of the independent or dependent variables; important in ensuring that any pattern is detected.

Reactant A substance we start with before a chemical reaction takes place.

Reactivity series A list of elements in order of their reactivity. The most reactive element is put at the top of the list.

Reduction A reaction in which oxygen is removed (or electrons are gained).

Relationship The link between the variables that were investigated. These relationships may be: causal, i.e. changing x is the reason why y changes; by association, i.e. both x and y change at the same time, but the changes may both be caused by a third variable changing; by chance occurrence.

Relative atomic mass, A_r The average mass of the atoms of an element compared with carbon-12 (which is given a mass of exactly 12). The average mass must take into account the proportions of the naturally occurring isotopes of the element.

Relative formula mass, M_r The total of the relative atomic masses, added up in the ratio shown in the chemical formula, of a substance.

Repeatable A measurement is repeatable if the original experimenter repeats the investigation using same method and equipment and obtains the same results.

Reproducible A measurement is reproducible if the investigation is repeated by another person, or by using different equipment or techniques, and the same results are obtained.

Respiration The process by which food molecules are broken down to release energy for the cells.

Resolution This is the smallest change in the quantity being measured (input) of a measuring instrument that gives a perceptible change in the reading.

Retention time The time it takes a component in a mixture to pass through the column during gas chromatography.

Reversible reaction A reaction in which the products can re-form the reactants.

Risk The likelihood that a hazard will actually cause harm. We can reduce risk by identifying the hazard and doing something to protect against that hazard.

S

Salt A salt is a compound formed when some or all of the hydrogen in an acid is replaced by a metal (or by an ammonium ion). For example, potassium nitrate, KNO_3 (from nitric acid).

Saturated hydrocarbon Describes a hydrocarbon that contains as many hydrogen atoms as possible in each molecule.

Scale (limescale) The insoluble substance formed when temporary hard water is boiled.

Scum The precipitate formed when soap reacts with calcium and/or magnesium ions in hard water.

Shape memory alloy Mixture of metals which responds to changes in temperature.

Shell (or energy level) An area in an atom, around its nucleus, where the electrons are found.

Smart polymer Polymers that change in response to changes in their environment.

Smelting Heating a metal ore in order to extract its metal.

Soapless detergent A cleaning agent that does not produce scum when used with hard water.

Soft water Water containing no dissolved calcium and/or magnesium salts, so it easily forms a lather with soap.

Solid A state of matter.

Stainless steel A chromium-nickel alloy of steel which does not rust.

State symbol The abbreviations used in balanced symbol equations to show if reactants and products are solid (s), liquid (l), gas (g) or dissolved in water (aq).

Steel An alloy of iron with small amounts of carbon or other metals, such as nickel and chromium, added.

Sulfur dioxide A toxic gas whose formula is SO_2. It causes acid rain.

Symbol equation A balanced chemical equation showing the formula of each reactant and product in the reaction, e.g. $H_2 + Cl_2 \rightarrow 2HCl$

T

Tectonic plates The huge slabs of rock that make up the Earth's crust and top part of its mantle.

Temporary hard water Hard water which is softened when it is boiled.

Thermal decomposition The breakdown of a compound by heat.

Thermosetting polymer Polymer that can form extensive cross-linking between chains, resulting in rigid materials which are heat-resistant.

Thermosoftening polymer Polymer that forms plastics which can be softened by heat, then remoulded into different shapes as they cool down and set.

Titanium A shiny, corrosion-resistant metal used to make alloys.

Titration A method for measuring the volumes of two solutions that react together.

Transition element Element from the central block of the periodic table. It has typical metallic properties and forms a coloured compound.

Transition metal See Transition element.

Trial run Preliminary work that is often done to establish a suitable range or interval for the main investigation.

U

Universal indicator A mixture of indicators which can change through a range of colours depending on the pH of a solution. Its colour is matched to a pH number using a pH scale. It shows how strongly acidic or alkaline liquids and solutions are.

Unsaturated hydrocarbon A hydrocarbon whose molecules contains at least one carbon–carbon double bond.

Unsaturated oil Plant oil whose molecules contain at least one carbon–carbon double bond.

V

Valid Suitability of the investigative procedure to answer the question being asked.

Variable Physical, chemical or biological quantity or characteristic.

Variable – categoric Categoric variables have values that are labels. For example, names of plants or types of material.

Variable – continuous Can have values (called a quantity) that can be given by measurement (for example, light intensity, flow rate, etc.).

Variable – control A variable which may, in addition to the independent variable, affect the outcome of the investigation and therefore has to be kept constant or at least monitored.

Variable – dependent The variable for which the value is measured for each and every change in the independent variable.

Variable – independent The variable for which values are changed or selected by the investigator.

Vegetable oil Oil extracted from plants.

Viscosity The resistance of a liquid to flowing or the 'thickness' or resistance of a liquid to pouring.

W

Wind Moving air.

Word equation A way of describing what happens in a chemical reaction by showing the names of all reactants and the products they form.

Y

Yield See Percentage yield.

Index